In this book, Fredrica Halligan gives us generous insights from the great spiritual figures of the East and West—Ibn 'Arabi, Thomas Merton, Buddha, Thomas Keating, the Divine Mother, the Dalai Lama, and more. She shows that learning how to love leads to greater understanding among the world's major religions, a communal path to the mystical unity of all humanity.

Ewert Cousins, Ph.D.
General editor, *World Spirituality:
An Encyclopedic History of the Religious Quest*

Against a background of Jungian thought, Fredrica Halligan draws from Christianity, Buddhism, Sufism and Hinduism to explain the stages of mystical growth. Examples drawn from her counseling practice make the ideas concrete. This book is a source of wisdom and hope in a troubled world.

Cullene Bryant, D.Min.
Pastoral educator, Providence Health Care, Vancouver, BC

Fredrica Halligan has written this book from her own depths, heart to heart. Keenly and intelligently, she captures the essence of the spiritual journey in crystal clear language. Her words are alive, and they inspire hope and engender joy.

Murray Stein, Ph.D.
Author, *Transformation: Emergence of the Self*

With today's growing interest in a spirituality that transcends the historic traditions, people in increasing numbers are engaging in the exploration of mysticsm as a more common form of spiritual experience. In this book, Fredrica Halligan has described some fascinating dimensions of the task, focusing on 'a mysticsm for our postmodern age' and drawing on her extensive understanding of the psychology of religion and the phenomena of mystical experience.

Peter Laurence, Ed.D.
Co-editor, *Education as Transformation: Religious Pluralism,
Spirituality and a New Vision for Higher Education in America*

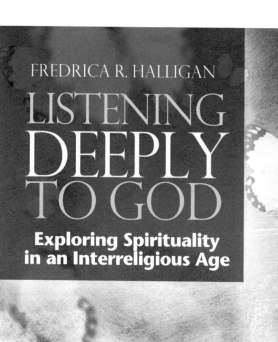

FREDRICA R. HALLIGAN

LISTENING DEEPLY TO GOD

Exploring Spirituality in an Interreligious Age

Twenty-Third Publications
A Division of Bayard
185 Willow Street
P.O. Box 180
Mystic, CT 06355
(860) 536-2611 or (800) 321-0411
www.twentythirdpublications.com
ISBN:1-58595-261-3

Published in Canada by Novalis
49 Front Street East, 2nd Floor
Toronto, Ontario, Canada
M5E 1B3
1-800-387-7164 or (416) 363-3303
E-mail: novalis@interlog.com
ISBN:2-89507-385-6

Library of Congress Catalog Card Number: 2002116015
Printed in the U.S.A.

Namaste.

This work is dedicated to all who will read it.

I pray that your spiritual practices will be

deepened, purified and strengthened.

May God bless you.

Dear Bob –
Many blessings on you
and your family! With
great gratitude for all
you have given.
In Divine Mother's Love!
Frederica

Table of Contents

Acknowledgments

I wish to express my deep gratitude to all those spiritual teachers and companions who have led me and served as my "Angels of the Heart": to Bob Tolz, Silvia Perera and Ewert Cousins who have personally guided me, to Janet Ruffing who has inspired me in the many hours of teaching together, to Peggy Levinson and Sastri Pappu who first introduced me to Sai Baba, to the members of Cafh who have companioned me in the mystical quest, and to many fine priests, nuns and lay people who have explored with me the deepest meanings of the Christian faith. Our dialogue over the years has been rich and fruitful. I owe gratitude also to my professors at Washington University in St. Louis where the study of Comparative Religion is deep and vibrant.

In producing this work, I am indebted to Bob Forman, Kitty Sample and Patsy Schumacher who read all or portions of the manuscript and offered helpful suggestions. And to my editor, Mary Carol Kendzia, publisher, Gwen Costello at Twenty-Third Publications, and commissioning editor, Kevin Burns at Novalis, I owe thanks. I am truly appreciative of the labor of love that has involved so many people in this statement of essential unity.

Introduction

My heart has become capable of every form:
it is a pasture for gazelles and a convent for Christian monks,
and a temple for idols and the Pilgrim's Ka'ba
and the tables of the Tora and the book of the Qur'an.
I follow the religion of Love: Whatever way Love's camels take,
that is my religion and my faith.

Ibn 'Arabi (1165–1240 CE)

The great mystics of every religion teach us the same universal message: the essence of life is love. God is love. We are created in love. Our task on earth is to live a life of love.

One of my favorite modern-day saints is Tom Wells. Until recently he was the pastor of a young Catholic parish in Maryland. Whenever he witnessed the marriage of a young couple, he would tell them in his homily: "I urge you—please, please, please—every day of your life get down on your knees and ask God to teach you how to love."

How to love: that is really what life is all about, isn't it? It's not an easy thing to learn. In fact, it is surprisingly difficult. It seems life continually sends challenges that remind us we still have more to learn about how to love.

If our primary task in life is to learn how to love, then who are the teachers who will guide us? As we think back over our lives, we usually remember some of those teachers. Many of us had good parents who loved us. Their task was probably easy enough when we were little and cute and acting lovable; not so easy when we were willful two-year-olds, four-year-olds, or rebellious teens. It was not so easy when they were tired, pressured, or low on money or other resources. But most of our parents tried hard and we learned a lot from them about how to hang in there and keep on loving when the going is difficult.

Some of us did not have such good parents, and then—especially then—we had to learn about love from other people. There are many sources where we learn about love: grandparents and siblings, teachers and scout leaders, coaches and music directors…the list goes on and on. I'm sure you can recall some of those special people in your life who taught you about love.

Sometimes we learn about love in churches or synagogues, mosques or temples. We learn about love in the words we hear in Scripture; but we only come to believe those words when we experience love surrounding us, permeating our very being.

If we think about God as the essence of love, and if we think about angels as being messengers of God, then it is not difficult to imagine angels as being those very special people in our lives who have loved us and who have taught us how to live our lives lovingly. These angels are the people who surround us, giving us intermittent gifts of love.

But God gives us internal as well as external resources. Every night we have dreams that teach and guide us. We may also have insights that arise spontaneously through meditation or prayer. I call these the internal messengers of God. All together these internal bits of wisdom are messages from what I have been led to call the "angel of the heart."

The most important lessons come, I think, from angels who are operating in both the external and internal dimensions of our lives. What I mean is that often the people who help us the most are those who teach us to listen to our internal messages. (Some therapists call this process "empowerment." I think of it as "mystical mentoring.")

The person who taught me the most about listening inwardly was a spiritually-oriented psychiatrist named Tomás Agosin. In the ten years I knew and worked with him, Tomás taught me how to listen and interpret the messages from my dreams, and how to let this inner wisdom guide my spiritual development and my life. From Tomás I learned to listen to the angel of my heart and let that inner angel teach me how to live lovingly.

Recently I have also learned a lot about internal angels through the writings of the great mystics from different religious traditions. I have come to appreciate both the cultural diversity and the exquisite similarities that occur in the mystical traditions of all the world religions. As one Native American spiritual leader said: "God loves diversity." When we look at the vast range of vegetation and animal life along with the full spectrum of human life, it seems he is right: God does love diversity. When we turn inward to listen to the angel of the heart, we learn how to be compassionate to the diversity that surrounds us.

Thomas Merton, the great Christian contemplative monk, went to India and Southeast Asia in 1968. There he had a powerful spiritual experience that taught him to transcend the differences of East and West. Standing alone and barefoot, gazing at the huge Buddha statues in the caves at Polonnaruwa in Ceylon (present-day Sri Lanka), Merton came to a deep sense of serenity and peacefulness. As noted in *The Asian Journal of Thomas Merton*, all the questions of theology melted away. He realized that "everything is compassion."

At some deep level the angel of his heart led him to know that God's love is beyond all the differences in religious traditions and above all the arguments about this or that—even the argument of whether there is a God or pure emptiness! In the face of that argument, Buddha was silent, and at Polonnaruwa Merton understood that silence:

> Then the silence of the extraordinary faces. The great smiles. Huge and yet subtle. Filled with every possibility, questioning nothing, knowing everything, rejecting nothing, the peace not of emotional resignation but of transcendence, of emptiness, that has seen through every question without trying to discredit anyone or anything—*without refutation*—without establishing some other argument.

Merton realized that such peace, such silence can be frightening "for the doctrinaire, the mind that needs well-established positions," but even that realization came with compassion. The seemingly endless arguments of liberals and conservatives, for example, need not be discredited or refuted. No need to argue about such things, Merton learned.

Merton was overcome by an experience that gave him "a rush of relief and thankfulness." He wrote,

> Looking at those figures I was suddenly, almost forcibly, jerked clean out of the habitual, half-tied vision of things, and an inner clearness, clarity, as if exploding from the rocks themselves, became evident and obvious.... The thing about all this is that there is no puzzle, no problem, and really no

"mystery." All problems are resolved and everything is clear, simply because what matters is clear. The rock, all matter, all life is charged…everything is emptiness and everything is compassion.

Merton called this experience an "aesthetic illumination" with such a sense of beauty and "spiritual validity" that it was beyond what he had known in his life before.

Thomas Merton, Tom Wells, Tomás Agosin: three deeply spiritual men, all coincidentally with the same first name. All three lived and died during the twentieth century. All three died suddenly and at a very early age (fifty-three, fifty-six, and forty-three respectively). All three lived active, generous lives and all three had authentically contemplative practices of prayer and meditation. Each one listened deeply to God and to the angel of his heart; each brought the fruit of that inner listening to many others. One a monk and writer, one a pastor, one a teacher and therapist; each lived a warmhearted, self-giving life and each touched many, many others with the gift of love.

In this small book, I endeavor to express what I have learned from the angel-messengers and the mystics I have encountered in my own life and in my studies. The psychology of religious experience and, in particular, the phenomena of mystical experience have been the focus of my interest. I trust the angel of the heart will guide me in this work.

.

CHAPTER ONE

The Making of a Mystic

How does one become a mystic? According to the Christian tradition, it involves a progression in our lives from purgation through illumination and into mystical union with God. Let's take a brief look at these three elements now.

In purgation, we strive to become aware of our sins, show sorrow for the past, and atone for offenses against God. As a psychotherapist, I shudder when I read what some of the medieval Christian mystics wrote about sinfulness. Their thoughts about self-accusation and abject contrition don't sit well with twentieth- and twenty-first-century psychological understanding of mental health or with our concerns about psychological guilt. In fact, some conditions, such as obsessive-compulsive disorder, are rooted in neurotic guilt. Sigmund Freud understood that, and it is one of the reasons he was so opposed to religion. But the spiritual directors of old knew it too: they called this condition "scrupulosity." They knew, as we know, that it is not healthy to beat oneself up continually or wallow in one's sense of inadequacy and sinfulness.

On the other hand, the mystics were right about the need for a process of purification. We really can't become deeply spiritual if our lives are ingrained with stealing, lying, cheating—or worse. If we are serious about progressing in our spiritual lives, we need to accept the likelihood that God will wean us (one way or another) from our bad habits. We will be called to truth, for example, because without a commitment to truth we will have a difficult time learning to love expansively the way the mystics do.

Illumination is enlightenment of the mind in the ways of God, as well as a clear understanding of God's will for us. In this regard, the angel of the heart, that internal message-giver, helps us understand our lives and, in particular, recognize the way in which divine energies permeate our reality. To the extent that we are able to receive this knowledge, the angel of the heart is ready to carry God's messages to us.

Mystical union may seem like a strange concept when we are just beginning our spiritual journey, but it is important to realize that this is our goal. Carl Jung, the noted Swiss psychiatrist, called the state of mystical union "conjunctio." He saw it as a process of finding our inner wholeness—the union of our masculine and feminine characteristics, for example. Others, especially the Jewish and Christian mystics, saw this union as a "mystical marriage" of the individual soul with God. They based their understanding on the Song of Songs, that great mystical love poem of the Bible. These mystics believed that if God truly loves us, and if God is wooing us through all the experiences of our lives, we can begin to turn towards God with full recognition that this is our true Beloved! This is the One for whom we long.

The aim of the spiritual journey is therefore this unitive consciousness. If we can accept that as our primary goal, then we will have oriented our lives toward a full realization of the mystical marriage with our Divine Beloved. We will need to trust that God will show us the way, that the angel of the heart will guide us.

I have been speaking of the angel of the heart in metaphorical terms. Likewise, many of the mystics found it easier to write in metaphors about their experiences. It is easier to talk about an angel than to describe experiences that are essentially ineffable. If it is helpful for you to picture an angel with wings, then do so; but for many of us, "angel" is essentially a term used to describe the way in which our journey to the divine is guided (or, in Buddhist terms, the way we become enlightened).

In describing some of the spiritual traditions of the major world religions, I do so as a psychologist seeking comparisons. In my study of these religions, I have noticed the many similarities in their various approaches to the spiritual quest. I do not mean to minimize the differences, remembering that God loves diversity. But I do think it is helpful to highlight the underlying unity in each of the spiritual traditions, as well as in the common themes the mystics of these various traditions use to describe their ascent towards divine wisdom and love.

In my spiritual quest, I have found the Sufi tradition to be particularly helpful. One of the leading mystical writers among the Sufis is Ibn 'Arabi, who was born in Spain in 1165 and died in Damascus in 1240. (That makes him a contemporary of St. Francis of Assisi in Christianity and Maimonides in the Jewish tradition.) Known among the Sufis as "the greatest master," Ibn 'Arabi writes eloquently about many facets of the mystic quest. His understanding is grounded in the Sufi idea of "unveiling." In *The Self-Disclosure of God: Principles of Ibn 'Arabi's Cosmology*, William Chittick writes that unveiling "is knowledge that God gives directly to the servants when he lifts the veil separating Himself from them and 'opens the door' to perception of invisible realities."

If we are the "servants" of God, then we are the ones waiting to have the veil lifted. Do we aspire to "perception of invisible realities"? Do we want to be "the folk of unveiling," that is, among those who are known as the highest ranking of the friends of God? These are questions each of us needs to ponder in our own hearts. How much do we want to see God? Do we have the longing to know the Divine? Do we desire to open ourselves to knowledge and union with the Beloved? Do we want to receive theophany?

Let's assume, for the moment, that we do have these desires—and to tell the truth, I think this really is the deepest desire of each one of us. If our desire is to know and to love God, then what is the likely route that we might travel if we pursue the path of mysticism? Ibn 'Arabi gives us some important clues, and we can watch for the ways in which the veils are lifted, one by one, as we travel the psychospiritual journey.

God is made manifest to us as we are ready to receive that gift. It can begin in a most ordinary fashion with our dreams. It is important to know that we all dream—whether we remember or not—on an average of five times each night. Although some neuroscientists claim that dreams are merely due to random fluctuations in the pons area of the brainstem, those of us who work personally and therapeutically with dreams know they are certainly not random, nor are they meaningless!

Our dreams are like windows into the world of the unconscious. The process of dreaming has many functions, one of which is to help us make connections between the day-to-day activities of our conscious life and the vast history of personal experience imbedded in our unconscious. There is also a deeper level to our dreams, which Carl Jung discovered and labeled "the collective unconscious." Here is where archetypal, universal themes appear. For example, themes such as relationship to authority and sibling rivalry connect us with our own personal experiences, but they also reflect universal experiences that others have had. (There are many archetypes and these are explicated in the many good books by Jungian dream analysts, some of which are listed in the resource section at the end of this book.)

Beyond the level of personal history and the archetypal level of the collective unconscious lies a deeper level sometimes called the mysterium. It is at this deeper level that the angel of the heart is working to reveal the divine mysteries to us. Here life is recognized as permeated by the divine. Here we see, with the mystics, that all life is sacred. Here we find abundant joy and all-encompassing love. Herein lies the innermost core of our being. The Immanent Divine resides within this space—"The kingdom of God is within you," is how Jesus said it. This is the realm we explore with the help of the angel of the heart. This is the realm we tap into when we listen most deeply.

The amazing things that the mystics reveal do not stop with the dreamlife, however. What Ibn 'Arabi writes about is found as well in all the spiritual traditions around the world: prophecy in dreams, voices heard, visions seen, the capacity to read thoughts. As mystics progress along the spiritual path, they appear to have a greater capacity to translate "from matter to spirit and from spirit to matter," as medieval spiritual seekers put it. This means there is a greater capacity to materialize concretely what is thought and felt and known in a spiritual manner.

In summary, from Ibn 'Arabi's perspective it appears that the making of a mystic may follow an evolution of consciousness, beginning with dreams, progressing to the appearance of dream-like images that appear fleetingly during wakefulness, then moving into voices—locutions—in which divine instructions are given, sometimes quite directly. When the mystic becomes more attuned to subtle messages, more surrendered and obedient to divine intent, the transmutation of spirit into matter may become increasingly concrete so that visions appear more full-bodied, more human, more "real" by ordinary standards. Further, Ibn 'Arabi tells us there is an opening of the heart wherein we may see God more clearly. As Sufi scholar Henry Corbin expresses it, we may progress to "vision of the heart, that is to say, vision through the inner eye...which is the vision of God by Himself, the heart being the organ, the 'eye' by which God sees Himself."

A contemplative life

The image of an "eye" within the heart is not as far-fetched as we might imagine. I once worked with a young woman in therapy who led a truly contemplative life. She was one of those rare individuals who had an ample amount of free time, which she chose to use contemplatively. I will call her Shelly (I have changed the names of the people mentioned in the case studies cited in this book). Silence and solitude were golden opportunities for Shelly; prayer and meditation were the avenues by which she communed with the Divine One centered in her heart.

During the course of our meetings, Shelly told me of her family history and of her bout with a serious, life-threatening illness. Was this struggle and time of suffering in her life part of the preparation for her deepened spiritual life? Together, we wondered about that. Shelly knew that her illness was a time of trust, a time of waiting and learning to surrender her life into the hands of the divine. She recognized her own essential powerlessness in the face of serious illness.

Shelly had read a great deal of mystical literature, especially that of the medieval Christian mystics. She knew that the theme of surrender of the ego is present in all the mystical traditions, both of the East and of the West. Surrender essentially means giving our life over to the divine will, relinquishing our desire to control and manipulate things according to our own preference. It means that we make God central in our lives. To live a surrendered life is not easy. It is a practice, a discipline. As Shelly worked to surrender more and more of her life, she deepened her spiritual commitment until it became central to her life.

In some ways, Shelly's story reads like a fairy tale come true. Not only was she healed of her illness, but she later married one of the healthcare workers who had been supportive of her. Too good to be true? In fact, it *is* true. Why was Shelly so blessed when others do not survive an illness such as hers? How are we to fathom such good fortune? What was in God's plan that carried her through the crisis? These are valid questions, not unlike the "why me?" questions people ask when their lives are less fortunate. But at a more profound level we can see that Shelly's life was evolving into an extraordinarily deep spiritual quest.

When I began to see Shelly in therapy, she had just been through two years where she had experienced profound feelings of blessedness. She felt enveloped in divine compassion, and she knew experientially the blessedness that is in life all around us. Prayer time was joy for her. She practiced centering prayer and found herself able to see God in all other beings. But then came the dark night.

Without any changes in her external world, Shelly suddenly felt spiritually bereft. "Where did it go?" she asked. She mourned the sense of blessedness that had been so nurturing for her. Prayer no longer felt enriching. Words and images simply would not come. Shelly spoke of how superficial life felt, especially when she was at social gatherings where other women focused primarily on materialistic pleasures. She found it difficult even to be charitable to such people when she was stripped of a sense of the divine in all things. Shelly knew she had to wait in stillness and last out this feeling of emptiness. Yet how was she to cope with this darkness?

Was she possibly depressed?

In working with Shelly it was immediately clear to me that she was not clinically depressed. Rather, she was in an interim period where she needed to let go of what she had already had and wait for whatever new would arise. During this time, she had a series of dreams that involved *breaking glass.* This image was symbolic of the shattering of the ego. Just as Shelly had to surrender and admit she was not in control of her illness, now she had to surrender and realize she was not in control of her spiritual life, either. In fact, it became clear that her spiritual life had a path of its own and that she was being directed to wait. One dream gave her a further directive: she was to put aside the books and attend to her own experiential process. So we waited and trusted. Her own spiritual process would emerge in its own way and its own time.

Emerge it did. On Easter morning of that year, Shelly sat on her deck meditating and taking in the beauty of trees and birds in the early springtime countryside. She felt a profound stillness and then a deep shift within her. She had great difficulty describing what happened. This is as close as she could come to expressing her experience: "*It was as if an eye had opened within me. It was a darkness that was light.*" A profound sense of rightness returned to Shelly. She knew she had been gifted in her spiritual life, and her joy returned. It was a quiet, humble joy, and Shelly talked of it as though she was cradling a fragile, very special gift.

"It was not an experience," she emphasized. I knew she meant that it was totally unlike any experience she—or I—had ever known. It was ineffable. Yet in our efforts to communicate with one another we had to find some words to use. I called it a "spiritual state" and Shelly accepted this wording, given that we both realized words were totally inadequate to encompass what had happened to her.

Shelly was fortunate to have a very fine spiritual director who was a contemplative monk in the Trappist order. He told her that the spiritual process she had experienced would continue: she would have periods of dryness and desolation, which would be followed by a deepening of her spiritual awareness.

I felt greatly privileged to have walked with Shelly through that particularly powerful time as the eye of her heart was opened. Shortly after this, we stopped our work together, as I was leaving the region where she lived. About a year later we talked on the phone, and Shelly told me, "It keeps going on and on."

Shelly had given me a modern-day glimpse into the mystical phenomenon that Ibn 'Arabi called "the eye of the heart." This is where, for Ibn 'Arabi, "God sees Himself," and we are merely the witnesses. This is where we know, truly and deeply, that God resides within our hearts. When that eye opens, we know. The dark and the light are united. The human and the Divine become One.

CHAPTER TWO

Encountering the Dark Side

It is alluring to read the stories of the great mystics when they write about their ecstasies and their joyful unitive states. We do not have to read far, however, to realize that such states are seldom handed to people unprepared. There is usually a long period of preparation at a conscious or unconscious level, a time that is often painful.

In writing about the spiritual development that occurs through the use of centering prayer, Thomas Keating says that we must work through the psychological layers of what he calls "the false self." We prefer to think of ourselves as all good; this pretense is what Jung calls "persona" and Keating refers to as the false self. Yet this persona, this false self, is not the true person we were meant to be. As noted in the previous chapter, before we can make progress into the realm of illumination and mystical delight, we must go through the purgation. We must know ourselves, our own inner darkness as well as our struggles and genuine giftedness. Carl Jung called this dark terrain the "shadow." In Jung's terminology, shadow and persona are both archetypes, by which he means that these phenomena are universal.

Shadow is what we would rather not know about ourselves. We all have areas within our psyches of which we are deeply ashamed, and we tend to disavow any knowledge of this dark terrain. In psychotherapy we often journey into the underworld of the shadow. While it may be painful, we need to look honestly at what is not pretty. We cannot know ourselves fully unless we can admit to our prejudices, our pettiness, our irritability and grumpiness, our rages, our sense of entitlement, our feelings of worthlessness and, above all, our shame. Each individual is different, of course, but each of us has a deep, dark area of shame that we hide from the world.

Dee was a woman with whom I worked in psychotherapy. She was bright and attractive, with a lovely smile and a pleasing personality. She was popular among her friends and very capable as a manager in a human services agency. Dee never felt competent, however, and would come to therapy feeling bruised whenever anyone criticized her work or resisted her suggestions. She was good at analyzing the organization and she could see where changes were needed, but when her administrative work did not run smoothly she felt deeply wounded. Surely any administrator has to expect a certain amount of criticism and resistance, especially when there are changes in policy and procedures. Her difficulty in taking criticism led us to an exploration of her shadow.

Deep within her, Dee had a great abyss, an inner terrain where she felt worthless and inadequate. In exploring her personal history she discovered the roots of those feelings. Her self-esteem had been badly damaged because, in her family, girls were valued less than boys. Her older brothers used to tease her and sneer: "You're only a girl," pronounced "girrrl!". Her parents contributed to the problem because they gave more freedom to the boys and allowed them to live a rough-and-tumble lifestyle. As she was growing up, Dee felt deeply wounded by the inequality. Although she grew strong and competent in her efforts to compete with her brothers, she never really felt she could succeed. Deep in her psyche she believed her brothers' taunts and felt totally inadequate.

Much as she hated this hellish inward terrain, Dee needed to sit with these feelings and not run away from them. She needed to grapple with the inner demons that told her she was inadequate. Often she would try to run away from these feelings or pretend they did not exist. But then, with courage, she would come back to the abyss. In sitting there, she learned to befriend the darkness so that it did not have such devastating power over her. In learning to bring the unconscious feelings to the surface, she dramatically reduced their destructive power.

Ther terrain of the abyss

Alice Miller writes about the process of coming to understand the abyss. Most often loneliness is at the heart of the matter. In *Prisoners of Childhood*, Miller describes many situations where children are mistreated, even by well-meaning parents. There is an essential gap between what a child needs and wants and what he or she actually gets. Picture a toddler in a crib, crying for his mother. He wants to get up and play but mother is busy; she is talking on the phone and so for a while she just lets him cry. What happens to the child is that he feels "unloved." Then, in the child's global way of thinking, he feels he must be "unlovable." He cries harder, screaming "Mommy!" By the time his mother comes she is irritated at his noisy demands and so her response is somewhat less than loving. The child, deep in his psyche, feels even more unlovable. This is the beginning of the abyss.

This hellish terrain—this abyss—is feeling unloved and unlovable! We all have some of this hellish abyss within us. None of us had perfect parents; and even if they were nearly perfect, they could not have had time to meet all our needs or to satisfy all our infant desires. We all grow up a bit wounded. There are unresolved feelings of dependence within us, and these tend to accumulate in multiple layers of feeling worthless, which appear especially when we are criticized or rejected. If we are fortunate, as we grow older we learn to know our own abyss and cope with its devastating feelings by letting in the light of realism and spirituality.

Nightmares

Dreams may point us toward the areas in our lives where self-esteem has been damaged by the criticism and rejection of others. One of the primary purposes of dreams is to teach us about ourselves. This is done when the dream brings feelings to the surface. Dreams show us in symbolic fashion what is occurring deep within our psyche. The feelings or emotions in the dream are the connecting link between our conscious and unconscious ways of knowing. When a dream portrays a particular feeling we can ask, "Where in my life right now am I feeling this way?"

There is a wide variety of dreams and many diverse ways to interpret them. One type of dream that is easy to recognize is a nightmare. These dreams are full of anxiety, pressure, and frustrations. Most of us do not like having nightmares, but we need to realize that these "negative" dreams have much to teach us.

Here is one such dream. You may recognize the all-too-familiar situations of being unable to complete a task and unable to get the help that is sorely needed to do so.

I was trying to write an exam and the time was short. I was also supposed to take care of my baby girl. My husband agreed to take care of the baby and I sat down at the computer in the school library. I typed for a while but time was running short. All the other students had left already. I pushed the button to get the disk out of the machine in order to print out the paper and hand it in. The disk came out but I could not find out where to print it. I went from machine to machine. With some I couldn't find the number buttons. With one I pushed the but-

ton to eject the disk and several disks came out along with much of the inner mechanics of the computer. It was a mechanical mess. I was getting more and more frustrated and couldn't find anyone to help me.

A young woman was up a ladder but she was not the computer assistant. A young man was in a chair with a sign saying that he was an instructor but he was busy and he brushed me off. He couldn't be bothered with inquiries. One machine would read letters and numbers but I had a bankbook and a long roll of sales slips that was all tangled. I was confused. I tried to find my disk and couldn't find what machine I had left it in. Then I tried to find my baby and she too was lost. I saw other people's babies but not my own.

It was ten o'clock and the library was about to close. I went to my husband for help. He was smoking a pipe instead of his usual cigarette. When he saw me, he hurried to leave. He was very critical, saying I was taking too long. He did not want to babysit anymore, and he didn't care a bit about my disk being lost or my exam being late. I pleaded with him but to no avail. "Please…please…please," but he just turned away from me in his stormy fashion.

Like most nightmares, this is a hellish dream, one of frustration, anxiety, thwarted competence, and above all, rejection. The woman who had this dream felt guilty about leaving her child, but she also felt thwarted in her academic efforts. Above all, she felt rejected by her husband. She felt that her legitimate dependency needs were shunned, and she felt emotionally abandoned. This is the terrain of the abyss.

Healing

Layer upon layer, our life experiences build up the complexes within our psyches, beginning in childhood. Clearing out this mess can be likened to the task faced by Hercules when told to clean out the Augean stables in a day. A whole river needs to be diverted to wash away the manure of our accumulated negative life experiences. Sometimes, the spiritual path itself can provide the water that washes away the manure. When our spiritual life contains the sense that we are loved by a beneficent God, then it is the "living water" that cleanses our soul and heals our wounds. What we all so desperately need is what a true spiritual path brings: a sense of being totally loved, just as we are.

Psychotherapy can also provide healing waters. Not everyone has the benefit of in-depth psychotherapy, however. Many times friends can be helpful for us in the same way that therapists can, if they are able to listen attentively and refrain from being judgmental. Friends can also be trained as co-counselors for one another and this can be very valuable. But in truth, unless they are trained as counselors, few friends are able—or willing—to sit with us when we feel abandoned, needy, or inadequate. Fortunately there is another widely available alternative; that is, our dreams. These can show us what we are dealing with as we struggle with our own abyss.

Out of the hell of inadequacy, abandonment, and rejection, we yearn to be cleansed and drawn into a spiritual life of love. Here the angel of the heart becomes the healer, the one who guides us. This internal messenger brings us first the dreams or the experiences that help us to see and fully experience the abyss. We need to listen deeply when we are guided to this therapeutically rich but often painful terrain. Then the angel of the heart diverts the waters that clean out the messy stables of our psyches. Our essential lovableness can truly be experienced only when we fully acknowledge our human frailty and our neediness.

So, in grappling with our shadow, what most of us need is to sit with the abyss—the loneliness, the feelings of being unloved and unlovable. We need to recognize how our history and personal life story can leave us feeling bereft, as well as how we develop feelings of low self-esteem, inadequacy, worthlessness, and fears of being "found out" as an "impostor." We also need someone who accepts us to accompany us into this terrain so we will come to the essential belief that we are lovable and know we are loved.

To hell and back

In some cases, the trip into the hellish underworld and back again may be a long and difficult one, fraught with dangers. Depending on our actual life experiences, we may have a great deal of "hell" that we need to uncover. I think here of Sister Catherine, a nun I once worked with. Our time together was a long, slow process that uncovered a history of incredible abuse. In cases such as hers a well-trained psychotherapist is essential.

Catherine came to me because she was blocked in her efforts to learn how to be a pastoral counselor and spiritual director. She was a pleasant woman and cared about others, but she was quite defensive and resistant to talking about herself. At first, Catherine said that she did not remember much about her childhood. I realized that she gradually needed to build trust both in me as her therapist and in the process of unfolding her life experience.

Sr. Catherine's dreams were very helpful in keeping us on track. She developed a knack for extending the dreamwork by depicting the key dream images in paints or magic marker drawings. I well recall one of her initial pictures where she drew herself in a small, single-person *armored tank* with slits for her to see out. A *tear was falling out of an eyehole.* As we looked at the picture together, we both saw that despite her armor-like defenses, her feelings were starting to break through. I felt grateful for the trust she was beginning to place in me.

Long before we knew the extent of her actual abuse, there were other clues as to the extraordinary pain Catherine had undergone. One of her dream images showed a *crucified child*, wrapped in swaddling clothes but hanging on a cross. This picture well-symbolized her story. As the memories began to emerge, she dreamt that she was *"raped by the king."* Then realistic memories started to surface: with horror Catherine remembered that as a four-year-old, she had been raped by her eighteen-year-old brother. More and more memories surfaced over a period of many months. Gradually, fearfully, she related scenes of gang rape, horror, torture, and intimidation. During her childhood, Catherine never felt safe. She was raped by multiple family members and forced into prostitution by her father.

Over the four-year period we worked together, the whole sordid history emerged. As her therapist, I felt horrified by what Catherine was uncovering. Both of us felt enormous compassion for this tragic "crucified child." Catherine's desolation and fear were completely understandable. I could never have imagined such a life story, especially for a nun! Hers was truly a case of having lived through hell.

Within psychology today, there is some controversy over the issue of repressed memories. Dr. Elizabeth Loftus is a psychologist who claims that all repressed memories actually form what she calls a "false memory syndrome," which is created, she feels, by therapists implanting suggestions in the minds of patients. Although it is true that false memories could in fact be implanted by the misuse of techniques such as hypnotic suggestion, it is not true that all repressed memories are false. Cases such as Catherine's have been helped by many well-trained therapists who are scrupulously careful not to implant suggestions or "lead the witness."

How does someone survive the horrors Catherine experienced? Even more remarkably, how could anyone do such horrible things to another human being? As I worked with Catherine, I felt a strong sense that what had been done to her was pure evil. This was the dark side at its most palpable intensity.

Therapists and scientists who have studied and worked with child abusers have learned that, most often, the perpetrators were themselves abused as children. The "evil geniuses" of history— Hitler and Stalin, among others—fall into this category. What happens in the mind of one who perpetrates abuse is a long and complex story, and beyond the scope of this book. Suffice it to say that rage and cruel aggression are defensive maneuvers. One who has been seriously hurt himself may identify with the aggressor. In this way he too becomes sadistic. Then whenever he is confronted by situations that make him feel belittled or humiliated, he lashes out aggressively. "I am not worthless," he asserts. "Rather, I am superior. I am powerful and I can prove it by showing my power to destroy others." Most likely, this was the dynamic operative in the minds of Catherine's abusers.

So how did she survive? And how did she become a caring person rather than an abuser herself? Catherine survived by looking at the light—literally. She recalled that in the small basement room where she was abused in earliest childhood, there was an overhead light bulb. While she was being raped she used to look at the bare light bulb and dissociate, that is, take herself out of her body in a process of self-hypnosis. Years later she found that "light" became a significant aspect of her spirituality.

Catherine also survived because of the support she received in school. Although no one knew what she was going through, the nuns in the Catholic school she attended were kind to her. Catherine was bright and the nuns helped her to achieve her utmost potential. It is no wonder that she herself became a nun, leaving home as soon as she was able and escaping to the safety of life in the church.

Catherine's story unfolded as more and more memories surfaced. After about three years we had a hint of the spiritual resources that had sustained her during the abuse. A dream showed her an image of *a huge robed monk holding a child.* "It was St. Anthony," she said. "He is the protector of children." We can easily surmise that when she was going through the horrors and tortures of her childhood, she imagined herself in the arms of St. Anthony, a protector of great strength and goodness. So, for her, St. Anthony was an angel of the heart. He sustained her psychologically while she went through the tragic abuse.

As Catherine was preparing to terminate therapy with me after four years of working together, another beneficent figure emerged in her dream. She called it *an angel of light,* and she knew it was associated with resurrection. She painted its picture in rainbow hues, standing straight and strong with great white wings spread out to the sides. This dream figure marked an important transition in her life. She had come through her hell, recovered her essential memories, and was well into recovery. Her angel of light offered her the promise of the triumph of spiritual strength even over darkness and evil.

Forgiveness

When entering the terrain of the abyss we find the dark truths that hold the psyche imprisoned. Until the psychological manure of our Augean stables is cleared out, we are not really free to go about our lives unencumbered. We have to understand the tragedies and misfortunes of our lives in order to let them go and get on with the business of living a loving life. Often we need to forgive those who have hurt us. Almost always we need to forgive ourselves as well.

Forgiveness is not something we can easily will to happen. Rather it is the end result of a process that is centered on understanding. First and foremost, we must understand what happened. All our own feelings and experiences need to be recalled and understood. Then, if possible, we need to understand—or at least imagine clearly—what was going on in the mind of the other person(s). Was he or she wounded somehow? What was the pain that generated this core of abuse? What patterns may have been acted out generation after generation? When the larger questions and issues are understood, then forgiveness can quite naturally occur. Tomás Agosin wrote:

> In forgiveness the ego becomes conscious of its limitations and imperfections, making itself vulnerable and humble. What happens to us when we go through this experience of forgiveness? What are we left with? What has happened within? First of all, forgiveness clearly has a redeeming quality....All too often, as we know very well from clinical experience, the ones who have been abused are the ones who abuse others....The victimized become the victimizers, continuing an endless chain of hurt, from generation to generation, to generation. Only with the recognition of that hurt and the full experience of that pain, can the transformation of forgiveness come about.

To stop the chain of victimization is something that applies to all of us. We need, for example, to forgive our parents so that we do not repeat with our children the hurt that was inflicted on us. In order to do this, we need to recognize that our parents also had been hurt. We empathize with them and come to understand them. Perhaps all therapy can be understood as a forgiving of the failings of our parents and others we have loved, so that we are free to love. Thus forgiveness redeems....

It is in the recognition of our limitations and our darkness that we find the light of love. Only when we face and embrace aspects we find unacceptable can we feel unconditionally acceptable. It is that state of our soul that opens our hearts to the deepest love, connecting us with all human beings, bar none.

In a case such as Catherine's, the abuse history was so violent, so powerful and so malignant, it was not possible for her to come to forgiveness during the four-year period of her therapy. But the work continues after therapy and Catherine came to some resolution before her death. She was able to say: "It is not mine to forgive." By this she meant that perhaps God could forgive her abusers even when she could not.

I heard recently that Catherine had died of a heart attack at the age of fifty-three. She had devoted her adult life to helping children. Perhaps the story of her survival will bring hope to other victims. Sister Catherine's story suggests that there is an angel of resurrection to guide each soul as she or he emerges from the abyss. As a therapist who has watched and facilitated many people in recovery, I too ally myself with this inner guide. I listen, and teach my clients to listen for the inner guidance that leads ultimately toward health and spiritual transformation.

Our own abyss can be scary enough, but most of us need not grapple with anything like the intensity of a story such as Catherine's. Yet like her, by entering into our own abyss, we can be freed from the abuses of our past and become far more capable of loving others. We can become more compassionate people. While we are in the dark terrain, sitting with the abyss, we must remember that, although this abyss may seem endless and global, it is not. There are other areas of the psyche and other aspects of life that are full of light. We come to fuller appreciation of the light once we have courageously looked at the darkness.

As Tomás Agosin once said: "When we sit in the abyss we come to appreciate there is a Divine Mother who is present there with us. She is waiting to comfort us." Despite the loneliness and fear of being unloved and unlovable, there are powerful forces of goodness that overcome darkness. By whatever name we call them—the angel of light, angel of resurrection, Divine Mother, angel of the heart—these are the messengers of the Divine Source that sustains us. Out of the darkness we come back into the light.

CHAPTER THREE

The Dreamworld

The illuminative aspect of our spiritual journey is greatly enhanced if we learn to recognize the messages given to us by our dreams. Our dreamlife is an imaginative wonderland. As bizarre as some dreams may appear, the dreamworld is not random; above all, it is not meaningless. Rather, dreams build on personal history and significant current happenings (which are often represented symbolically), and they point to future directions. They may also contain elements of a call or vocation from the Divine Source. Some dreams may appear to foretell the future but, as Jungian analyst Murray Stein notes, we cannot identify those rare precognitive dreams until after the event they have foretold has actually happened.

Working with dreams can be fascinating and complex, and there are many good books available to help you learn about the process, some of which are listed in the resource section of this book. Of the many ways to work with dreams, I find the Jungian approach to be the most comprehensive and helpful, and the one most likely to tap into the spiritual domain.

In general, our dreams address a few key questions:

• Who am I?
• How is God being revealed to me?

• Where am I going?
• When do I need to make the next move?
• What is expected of me?
• How am I being drawn to love, that is, to relate to others?

Of these, the basic question addressed by the Jungian approach to dreamwork is, "Who am I?" Jung discovered that dreams can help us to understand the multifaceted personalities we all carry. *Ordinarily we can look at every aspect of our dreams as an aspect of ourselves.* This may seem radical at first, but if you try it you might be amazed at how productive this technique can be for the process of self-understanding.

In the last chapter we discussed the importance of becoming aware of the negative aspects of our lives, including both what has happened to us in the past as well as our faults and shortcomings. This awareness can be helped by the images in our dreams. For example, a woman dreams of her mother-in-law, who is a very controlling woman. "Oh," she says with a shudder, "that's a shadow figure for me." But if she recognizes the "controlling woman" as an aspect of her own personality, she can then modulate that characteristic. When we are conscious of these negative aspects of our personalities, they are far less likely to get out of control and become problems in our relationships.

Jung pointed out that we also have both male and female characteristics within us. These are the inner characteristics for which Jung coined the terms "animus" (male characteristics in a female) and "anima" (female characteristics within a male). If you are female you might wonder: what kind of an animus do I carry? Is he authoritarian, protective, a good businessman, a scientist, or perhaps an artist?

Often the characteristics that constellate into a woman's animus are found in the father figures of her life; these can prove useful in certain circumstances of life. I recall that shortly after I was widowed, the image of a businessman came to me in a dream. For me, this figure represented a personal resource or characteristic that had been unconscious until then, but which was needed at that point in my life. It was a time when I was swamped by paperwork ranging from medical claim forms to taxes and investment options. Whenever I felt overwhelmed by all these business decisions, I called up the image of my businessman animus and asked him to accompany me as I worked.

In complementary fashion, a male dreamer may receive an image of his kindly, gentle anima just at a time when he most needs to bring forth his sensitive, relational qualities. Jung used to say that a man's anima will lead him to God, and he frequently used the example of Beatrice, Dante's guide, in describing the role and potentialities of the anima in a man's life. A man's mother figure (or figures) forms a template for his anima, however, so she may have shrewish rather than nurturing qualities, depending on the personality of the mother.

We all take on various roles in the dramas of life. How authentic are these roles to our actual, underlying personality? Conversely, how much artificiality do our roles portray? We may begin to discover our persona if we notice a dream figure who is hiding behind a screen or mask of some sort. If we put on a pretense of openness and kindheartedness while we hide a great deal of hostility, then we are not being authentic but hiding behind a mask of illusory beneficence. Watching political candidates address the public before an election is a good way to observe the nature of each candidate's persona. How she or he behaves once elected is more a measure of the values that have been motivating that person all along.

An example of a persona figure appearing in a dream is found in this account from a female professor: "*I was helping with a political campaign. A young woman was elected. She proceeded to stand at a large table in an inn, baking bread for the public.*" Through this dream, the woman realized that she herself needed to project a nurturing role in her image as a teacher. She tried this approach and had a successful year with both her students and colleagues at school.

Animus, anima, persona, and shadow are among the key archetypes that Jung recognized as occurring in the collective unconscious. They typically appear in dreams with great individual variability of images. In addition, dreamwork may reveal other archetypes that are common to the human psyche, across all cultures and all time periods. These archetypes include the trickster, the wise old one (male or female), the divine child, the seducer or seductress, the warrior, the monarch, the shaman. Also, any of the gods and goddesses from mythology, whether Greek, Roman, or of other cultures, may be interpreted as archetypes that reside within the human soul.

Recognizing the Self

By far the most significant archetype described by Jung is the one he called the "Self." This archetype can be defined as the sacred inner wholeness, the union of opposites or conjunctio. Self is therefore the inner marriage of our masculine and feminine characteristics, as well as of our persona and shadow. All conceivable opposites in our personalities are united in the Self. According to some Jungian analysts, Self is the Immanent Divine within the psyche, or the element of the psyche that knows the divine. Self is the center of the complete conscious and unconscious aspects of ourselves.

Self is different from "ego," which is merely the center of our conscious personalities. Ego is the "I" or the "me" of ordinary consciousness. Ego is the "I" that says: "I woke up this morning," "I went to work," "I am a mother (or father), architect (or banker)," or any of the other identifications in our conscious life. It is important to understand the difference between ego and Self because, as we shall soon see, ego must surrender in order for the true, spiritual Self to reign in one's personality. This is an essential step along the path of psychospiritual growth and development. Jung writes that this transition occurs most naturally at midlife (that is, at age thirty-five or beyond) and it usually comes about as a result of a personal crisis of some sort.

According to Jung, archetypal dreams can readily be identified whenever we encounter something that is clearly not of our own culture or personal history. Dreams of an ancient text, for example, or a shaman, an Indian princess, the Himalayas, or the Ganges, are examples of crosscultural dreams that alert us to information coming from the collective unconscious. From his extensive studies of various cultures and peoples, Jung found that dreams of Self were often expressed in mandala form: a circle, a square, or a quartered figure. The Self is also represented by the number four and multiples of fours, and by centering figures such as a great tree, a mountain, or a column, all of which represent the *axis mundi* or central pivot of the world.

Other special Self symbols include a beneficent figure of the same sex as the dreamer or a symbol of personal authority or centeredness, e.g., the Queen of England, the president, an orchestra conductor, Central Park, Grand Central Station, Center City, Rome, Jerusalem, Mecca, Mount Kilimanjaro, Mount Fuji, and so forth. Strangely enough, "a great fish" also represents Self. The Christ figure, says Jung, is a manifestation of the Self archetype in the collective unconscious.

Symbols of wholeness and individuation occurred in a dream of

Maria, a young student who was trying to decide on her college major. Her parents had emigrated from Italy to New York before she was born, and they maintained the Italian language and culture in their home. Maria had been working diligently to become Americanized. She was somewhat reluctant to live at home because that meant she did not have some of the social advantages—as well as the temptations—of life in the university residence halls. Nonetheless, Maria was actively involved with campus affairs.

When the time came to choose her major she considered language studies, specializing in Italian. She knew she could succeed in Italian but she was afraid she might be selling out her own individuality. She did not want simply to capitulate to her parents' wishes. Then a dream came:

> *I was in Rome at the square where Trajan's column stands. The column was larger, with a greater circumference, than in reality. It had the whole history of Rome sculpted around it, spiralwise, in bas relief. At the four corners of the square there were smaller columns, each with a lantern on top of it. A woman in white appeared and invited me to enter a doorway that opened into the column.*

Maria awoke with a sense of awe and numinosity, feeling that she had been in the presence of the divine. She described the dream and the woman in white as very vivid and very beautiful. She realized she was being called to a greater depth in her studies of Italian culture. Here was a Self figure who showed her that the path of her own individuation was indeed within the cultural heritage of her Italian background.

This dream was archetypal in its crosscultural symbolism and, in particular, in its historical context as Trajan's column specifically depicts the history of Rome. This is also a Self dream because of the emphasis on the square, the column—an *axis mundi*—the four lanterns, and the mysterious woman in white. This woman was clearly a beneficent figure, one who showed the way. In this dream the Self resolved Maria's inner conflict by pointing out that her own individuality was to be found by entering into the cultural heritage of her ethnic group. After this dream Maria happily declared her major in Italian, no longer afraid that she was "selling out" to her parents' wishes. She could sense "This is who I am," her own path of individuation, guided and affirmed by her dream.

Another example of a Self dream occurred in a crosscultural context that was totally unlike the dreamer's own ethnic background. This dreamer reported:

> *I dreamt I was traveling around the Mediterranean Sea. I saw it as if I was looking at a map from above. I traveled from Egypt westward across Africa, across the strait of Gibraltar and then eastward. I passed Rome where my parish priest was saying Mass, and I kept on going. I finally ended up in Iran where I encountered quite a junk pile. I began to rummage amidst the junk and unearthed a strange icon. It was a small, wizened old head with pine cones for the ears. I had a strong sense that this was a very sacred icon. With delight I showed it to a friend of mine, but she was a very critical woman and she saw no value in it at all. I knew she was wrong.*

Here the sense of numinosity is key. Although the critical shadow figure (the friend) doesn't understand, the dreamer knows she has unearthed a sacred figure, a god-image. It is the feeling of sacredness that reveals the dream's truth: in the very "junk pile" of life, the sacred is to be found! Wisdom comes through an appreciation of the holiness of ordinary things. The dreamer remembered this dream and, after many years, she finally discovered the meaning of the pine cone ears. She told me: "I realized I was to listen to the whispering of the pines. In nature, amidst the pines, I could clearly 'hear' the messages from the divine." One might say that, for her, the pines served as an angel of the heart, bringing seed thoughts that could guide her psychospiritual growth.

There is considerable overlap between what Jung calls Self dreams and the numinous dreams that would be identified as god-image dreams; the "god-head in the junk pile" is one such dream. The dream points to the core Self as well as to the sacredness that underlies all of life, the Immanent Divine in the dreamer and in all else. The dream's occurrence "in Iran" suggests the outlook of the Sufis, the Islamic mystics found in Iran and throughout the Mediterranean world, especially to the south and east of that sea.

Revelation

The second question we can ask of the dreamworld is this: how is God being made manifest to me? Those who are on a spiritual quest will be given periodic dreams that affirm and guide the search for the Divine One.

Some years ago, I had taken a month-long sabbatical during which I studied the writings of Thomas Merton, especially his later explorations of Muslim, Hindu, and Buddhist forms of spirituality. I had been reading *The Asian Journal of Thomas Merton*, as well as some of the same books Merton was reading during his travels in India and Southeast Asia. Shortly before his accidental death in Bangkok, Merton had a unitive experience in which he gained insights that transcended the differences between East and West. With Merton's explorations strongly imprinted in my mind, my own dream of unity emerged.

My dream began during sleep at about 2:30 in the morning, but it continued as I woke up. It was very vivid and very beautiful. I can best describe it as a "collage wall of worship." The wall was covered with figures, some actual people and some works of art. The pictures kept changing but I knew they were all sacred. Lao Tzu was there, the Dalai Lama, Our Lady of Guadalupe and Ishtar, Ramakrishna and Kali, many others I didn't recognize.

The sense of the sacred was palpable. The soft colors and intense beauty of the images added to my sense of wonder. The dynamism was also profound. Images gently flashed on and off again and gradually changed over time

When I awoke I felt great awe, and a wondrous sense of the myriad ways in which the Divine One is made manifest to us in different cultures down through the ages. I felt deeply grateful for the multiple manifestations that had been shown to me. My dream did not contain a simple, single god-image but a whole host of god-images, gods and goddesses who were united and ever-changing. What those images said to me was that God is dynamic and multifaceted. Across cultures and time periods, the Divine One is neither static nor rigid. Rather, there is a marvelous diversity in the myriad ways the divine is revealed to us. This is the realm of the mysterium.

In working with our dreams, we can find help from a variety of sources. Jungians and other psychotherapists, including Freudian and Gestalt therapists, work with dreams from the perspective of learning who we are. Mystics of all religious traditions look at dreams in terms of their capability to show us the divine.

Guidance

Another aspect of the dreamworld is prophetic or vocational. Jung would call this aspect the teleological pull of the Self, meaning that the Self pulls us along toward our true, essential wholeness; the Self guides our path of individuation.

At each step of our lives, especially at each crossroad or bend in the path, we may receive dreams that show us where we are going, when we need to make the next move, and/or what is expected of us. These aspects of dreamlife are not only specific to the individual dreamer but are also very specific to the particular time and decisions that the dreamer may be encountering.

Where we are going is crucial to our decision-making. The old adage to "sleep on it" when there is an important decision to be made seems to recognize the value of dreams in sorting through options and coming to a clear decision. Dreams can also provide answers to questions that we ask in prayer, in meditation, or in the altered state of consciousness that we experience just before falling asleep. For this reason it is often helpful to use our pre-sleep time—even a few moments—for prayer or spiritual reading. This allows us to quiet our minds and bring ourselves into the deepest aspects of our psychospiritual selves.

The answers that are given at each crossroad in our lives often come in symbolic, imagistic ways. I recall a dream I once had when I was wondering whether to continue working with the Chilean psychiatrist Tomás Agosin. In my dream *a house with a Spanish-style red tile roof* was prominent, which symbolized Tomás's cultural heritage. At another decision point, I dreamt of *a hospital with round windows*, much like the windows in a hospital in Chicago where I had applied and been accepted for a post-doctoral residency.

Often we recognize these directional dreams by the clear sense of having made a decision. The last image of the dream and the first waking, conscious thought give the summary of the dream's conclusion. So even if we do not remember the whole dream, we have the essence of its wisdom in that final dream image and first waking thought. I have found these types of directional signals to be extremely valuable and trustworthy, and have never regretted a decision made on the basis of these clear directions.

At times people receive dream directions but do not heed them. I recall a college senior who was trying to decide whether to live at home after graduation as her parents wanted, whether to get an apartment with a friend, or whether to enter into marriage—a "green card marriage" with a young man who had proposed to her simply as a way of becoming a citizen of the United States. The young woman's parents were strongly opposed to the third option for many realistic reasons, but the student was leaning in that direction, in part to rebel against her parents but also because of her fear that she would never find anyone else to marry.

Shortly before graduation this young woman had a long, elaborate dream that told her quite clearly she should not marry the young man who had proposed to her. She disregarded the dream, strongly influenced by her ego-need to become a married woman, and she went ahead with plans for the marriage. Six months after graduation she called to tell me that she had been seriously injured in a car accident. It was only while recuperating in the hospital and realizing the near-fatal situation she had come through that this young woman decided to heed the dream and call off the inappropriate marriage. Shortly after making this decision she began dating another young man and was very happy about the direction she had finally chosen.

Surrender of the ego is an essential aspect of psychospiritual growth and development. Jung tells us these calls to surrender occur most often after midlife, and he says, "The ego must die for the Self to emerge." The young woman's ego wanted the green card marriage, but her Self—her inner wisdom—knew better. When we get clear directions from a dream to move in a wholesome, self-affirming manner, it is very unwise to disregard such messages.

In discerning the meaning of directional dreams we need to make use of our rational abilities and good common sense. Barry was a young man who led a committed Christian life. Strongly influenced by the charismatic movement, he genuinely offered his life to Jesus and was willing to make any sacrifice or go wherever God might be calling him. At the time, he was working as a special education teacher and he was much appreciated for his caring attitude. Then he began to have a series of dreams that showed *managers, management consultants,* and himself in *managerial roles.* He began to think that God might be calling him to move from teaching into some form of administration. He was willing to make the change, if that was what God wanted of him. At the same time, he realized that in fact he was not very good at managerial tasks. He tended to get anxious and confused when he had a lot of details to coordinate, and in his personal life he was quite disorganized.

Barry prayed about the dreams, asking Jesus if this was really what he was being called to do. Through prayer and listening to the angel of the heart, Barry realized that these management dreams were not vocational dreams, but personal dreams aimed at helping him find his own wholeness. Instead of being called to a career change, Barry was receiving inner help and guidance toward becoming a better manager in his personal life. With that realization, he happily set about organizing himself and getting his life in order.

Discerning the message

Like Barry, when we feel we may have had a dream that is giving us direction, we need to subject that possibility to careful scrutiny. We can ask ourselves questions such as "Does it make sense to move in that direction?" "Do I feel strongly that this is what God is calling me to do?" With openness and a willingness to surrender, we can count on our inner wisdom to guide us and prevent us from making serious mistakes.

Sometimes, we may be clear about our direction but unclear about the timing. Dreams may then tell us when we are to make the next move. Dreams that contain a message such as "You must wait upon the Lord" are telling the dreamer, "Not yet!" Then again, dreams tend to be quite specific about when to move ahead. Career moves may be directed in this way. For example, a dream may clearly tell us, "It's time to get out now; it will be much harder if you wait." Or, "I want you to leave in a year."

The pace of any activity may also be slowed down or accelerated by messages from the dreamworld. Recently, after receiving a message to write this current book, I had another dream with the message that I must get about the task promptly and with dispatch because "You won't have much time to do it in." So despite a heavy schedule, I planned a new morning routine. After a half-hour of meditation, I would begin my day with a few pages of writing.

Each of us has the potential to do many things. To be all that we are meant to be does not mean being perfect, however. Rather, living up to our potential means listening to our own inner guidance and developing the abilities that enable us to create our own unique selves. This is what Jung called the path of individuation.

Ibn 'Arabi, the twelfth-century Sufi mystic, lived a life that was totally surrendered to God. Toward the end of his life he had a visionary experience in which he was called to write a summary of the wisdom he had received. His book, *The Bezels of Wisdom*, was given to him prophetically. He writes,

> I saw the apostle of God in a visitation granted to me….He had in his hand a book and he said to me, "This is the book of *The Bezels of Wisdom*; take it and bring it to men that they

might benefit from it." I said, "All obedience is due to God and his Apostle; it shall be as we are commanded."

It was natural for Ibn 'Arabi to follow this call. All his life he strove to carry out what God expected of him. And so he set down the wisdom and messages he had received into the book, which is about many of the prophets in the Bible.

Joan of Arc is another great saint who followed her inner guidance. She is well-known for receiving messages that came to her as visions and voices (known as "locutions"). On the basis of these messages, Joan dressed herself in armor and led an army, whose mission was to free the Dauphin of France from British captivity and return him to the throne as the rightful king. The "Maid of Orleans," as the French called her, was discredited by the church and eventually burned to death as a heretic. She may not have fulfilled human expectations, but she was ultimately true to the expectations of God as she received them in her heart. Long after her death, the Catholic Church recognized her sanctity and canonized her. She is now known as a saint and martyr.

Ibn 'Arabi and Joan of Arc were great mystics and saintly leaders. Their lives were totally surrendered to God's will. It doesn't take a great saint, however, to live a life surrendered to God; all it takes is courage and trust. Like Barry, who was ready to surrender a career he loved, it takes willingness to try and discern God's will. In this effort, dreams can be a most helpful medium. Through dreams the angel of the heart whispers what is expected of us.

My own call to write this book came in a series of two dreams which I had on July 17, 2000. In all humility, I must listen and follow when I receive such a message. In the first dream,

I am in an historic building in a city like Washington, D.C. Some foreign students come to visit. They express their disgruntlement because their professors (of spirituality and Jungian studies)

have sent them to the city without adequate orientation. So I step into the gap. I'm willing to show them what I know, but I also give the caveat that I've only been here a few years and there's much I still don't know about the city.

We begin by looking at the corridor that surrounds a rotunda in the building. Then we go out on a porch roof that also surrounds the rotunda. From the roof we can see into the city, but it isn't an expansive view. I explain that we can't really get a picture of the whole from here. We'll have to go into the city in order to see, in more detail, its many significant places. So we begin our tour. First is a building that is very modern but which has been there for a while. Inside it has sleek, soaring metallic sides, sweeping up to the top. I admired the beauty of this building and its unique, ultramodern construction, and I helped the students to appreciate it as well.

At this point I awoke, wrote down the dream, and fell back asleep. In the second dream,

I am with a group of unknown people in a setting similar to the last dream. I hear a tour guide lecturing nearby. They leave to go to the third floor where there is an art gallery. I hurry along, wanting to hear what the lecturer is saying.

As I'm going up in the elevator, I realize I am in the process of writing a book. It is a slim volume of poetry. As the door opens at the third floor I know my book is a sequel to The Art of Coping *(my previous book), and that it is about the spirituality and dream chapters in that previous book. I realized I don't necessarily have to refer back to* The Art of Coping *but that I'm writing and expanding on what was expressed in those two chapters.*

As the elevator door opens I see a huge statue (triple or quadruple life-size) and I come out to do homage at her feet.

Then I know the name of the statue and the theme of the book: Angel of the Heart. I bow slightly and pray briefly, offering my efforts to the Divine Mother who is expressed here in the angel.

When I awoke from this dream I knew clearly: this is my call. This is my book and it must begin this very day. I do not know whether all authors receive their inspiration in dream form but that certainly has been the case for me. This is my third book, and each of the others also were inspired by direct dream messages.

There is much evidence of the creativity that flows from the unconscious during dreams. Both scientific and artistic creativity may occur in dreams. Certainly I was surprised and delighted to find my angel of the heart so clearly expressed in my dream. (I had never thought much about angels before this dream.) She is a numinous figure and one clearly deserving my homage. In following the expectations set forth for me in this pair of dreams, I see myself as one who is led and guided by this personification of the creative spirit; I see myself as "tour guide" to help readers and students explore a bit of this inner city as it has been shown to me.

A decision to love

The final question we must ask of our dream selves is this: how am I being drawn to love, to relate to others? On this theme we recall again what Ibn 'Arabi wrote: "My heart has become capable of every form….I follow the religion of Love: whatever way Love's camels take, that is my religion and my faith." Love is the essence; all the great spiritual masters agree on that. Unity of all humanity is the underlying mystical theme.

The contemporary Indian holy man Sri Sathya Sai Baba agrees. He says: "There is only one royal road for the spiritual journey…Love." He emphasizes this same universal theme when he writes: "There is only one race, the race of Mankind. There is only one religion, the religion of Love." These pronouncements of great mystics, past and present, echo the age-old commandments stated by Jesus: "You shall love the Lord your God with all your heart, and with all your soul, and with all your strength, and with all your mind; and your neighbor as yourself" (Luke 10:27). And again: "This is my commandment, that you love one another as I have loved you" (John 15:12).

The message is clear: our greatest call is to love God and to love one another. Yet, as we know, that call is not always easily fulfilled. There are multiple divisions within human society, and it is easy to get caught in a web of rejection and defensiveness. How can dreams help us to extricate ourselves from the tendency to criticize and reject one another? And how can dreams teach us to love? Dream researcher Montague Ullman writes:

> Our dreams confront us with the order and disorder that exists in our relationships with others and tell us something about their origins in earlier experience. Engaging in dream work in a social context provides the support we need to understand where we are as individuals in regard to this broader issue of "connectedness."...Our dream life addresses itself to the maintenance and repair of these connections by its capacity for honest display. It is as if that part of ourselves out of which these images flow is always in touch with the basic truth that, despite the fragmentation that has taken place among members of the human race down through history, we are still members of a single species....Confronted as we are now with the difficulty of managing our enormous destructive power, the question is: can we survive as a species without a greater investment in honesty and honest connection among nations?

Ullman is putting the dreamworld into the context of our need to survive as a human species. How can dreams help us in this regard? Is this their basic evolutionary purpose? He continues:

> Speculation along these lines makes me wonder if dreams are linked to a greater need, namely, that if we are to survive as a species we must do better than we have up to now in repairing the many ways we have ruptured connections between people. By unloading excessive and obstructive emotional baggage, by allowing ourselves to become more known, we achieve a greater freedom in human relationships and a greater respect for and tolerance of others....As we begin to deal more and more with the truth about ourselves, we increasingly recognize and discard self-deluding facades. I propose that what appears as collective dream work geared to the needs of the individual may, in fact, be linked to a deeper mechanism of species survival.

Ullman is making a very powerful inference here; that is, our God-given capacity to dream every night is so essential that our very survival depends on it. The nature of dreams is multifaceted: to take our present experience and integrate it with prior experiences; to look at the challenges of our daily existence in light of our call to live up to our full potential; to infuse our life with spirit when spirit is most needed; and to answer the prayer, as Tom Wells voiced it, "to teach us how to love."

Here is an example of a dream that corrected the course of action of the dreamer. The dreamer was a priest who was previously unaware of how his behavior was affecting others:

> *I was with a group of priests from my order. One of them, Fr. Joseph, is very critical by nature. (He's controlling and manipulative by criticizing anything that, in his eyes, falls short of perfection.) He was complaining vociferously and I could sense*

he was drawing me into a triangle situation with his parish assistant. Finally I had to tell him point blank, "I hate being between you and Sister." I knew that might anger him and he would be likely to turn his anger on me.

Sure enough, in the next scene of the dream he was criticizing me: my appearance, my presumed self-importance and haughtiness, my not following Jesuit norms. He said, "The Provincial would never have approved of that!" Finally I said to him, repeatedly with increasing volume: "Shut up; shut up, shut up!" I saw another Jesuit coming into the room so I said one more time in his hearing: "Shut up, Joseph!"

Since he understood the meaning of dreams, when the priest awoke he knew immediately that he was confronting his own shadow-critic. He was also, of course, confronting his own self-importance. He asked himself: why did I have this dream right now? He remembered that, just before going to bed the night before, he had completed a book review in which he had been overly critical. He had not even finished reading the book but had panned it as being unprofessional and incomplete. On the basis of this dream he realized he would have to revise his review. He went back to his computer, softened his language, and wrote a more neutral review, even including a few positive points that he gleaned from perusing parts of the book he had not previously read.

This dream confronted the dreamer with his own hubris and overly critical attitude. It asked, in essence, how would you like it if someone criticized you the way you criticized that book you just partially read? The dream reminded him of the Golden Rule: to treat others as you would like to be treated.

Dreams may sometimes point out other common habits that can be detrimental to relationships, that is, the tendency to complain or gossip. These forms of verbal communication, even the thoughts that underlie these patterns, can be damaging; and dreams confront us with our habits. The resulting awareness can help us to change.

Dreams can also point out positive ways to enhance our relationships with one another. This inner wisdom and guidance can be powerful and dramatic. Do we need to forgive someone? A dream may point this out by showing us themes of forgiveness. Whenever we get a series of dreams with the same repeated theme shown in various scenarios and contexts, we should ask: where is that theme operative or needed in my life right now?

Jung pointed out that dreams often reveal compensatory themes. Often our dreams will indicate that something in our lives is out of kilter, or that we have gone off course in our psychospiritual development. For example, a dream of flying and crashing could be taken as a caution against self-importance. This type of dream is a reminder of the old adage: "Pride goes before a fall." If we heed the dream, an actual "fall" may be avoided. The dream will have helped us to correct course and thereby improve our relationships with others.

CHAPTER FOUR

Emptiness

In our secular Western culture, "emptiness" is not a highly valued trait. We are taught that nature abhors a vacuum, and, by implication, so should we. We are taught that we should know where we are going, and if the unexpected comes along, we should alter our plans and begin anew. But the wisdom of the mystics and the wisdom of the East teach an entirely different way of being. For example, in the thirteenth century the Persian poet and mystic Rumi wrote,

> Try to be a sheet of paper with nothing on it.
> Be a spot of ground where nothing is growing,
> Where something might be planted,
> A seed, possibly, from the Absolute.

Hayao Kawai, the first Jungian analyst in Japan, was intimately aware of both Eastern and Western values and ways of knowing. He taught that the Japanese mind is completely centered on the experience of emptiness. Whereas in the West the Jungian ideas of Self and fullness are at the center of one's being, in the East the center is sacred because of its emptiness. For example, Japanese schoolchildren spend nine years of their formative primary education practicing how to paint bamboo stalks and leaves. This activity is not just an exercise in calligraphy or a demand for perfection;

rather, it is a meditative practice that teaches emptiness. The belief is that when one is sufficiently empty the hand moves on its own or, as a Western mystic might put it, the brush paints but it is the unseen hand of the Divine that moves the brush.

A similar concept is found among the Sufis: God is the one who writes; God is the unseen hand that moves the pen. We can apply this concept to all human activity. In another, similar metaphor, God is the archer, while we are the bow or the arrow. As Kahlil Gibran has so beautifully expressed it in his poem, "On Children," found in *The Prophet*:

> You are the bow from which your children as living arrows
> are sent forth.
> The Archer sees the mark upon the path of the infinite,
> and He bends you with His might that His arrow
> may go swift and far.
> Let your bending in the Archer's hand be for gladness;
> For even as He loves the arrow that flies,
> So He loves also the bow that is stable.

An essential teaching in a spirituality of emptiness is that we are merely instruments in the hand of God. In emptiness we let go of our plans, our strident efforts; we let go of our pride or shame in regard to our accomplishments or failures. The past is relinquished and with it judgments about self-worth. So too, the future is relinquished along with our sense of ego-control and self-determination. We remain in the present moment and we remain open, like a blank sheet of paper, waiting to see what God will do with us next.

There is an ancient prayer that invites this kind of emptiness and essential openness to divine action:

I adore Thee, Divine Mother,
and I offer Thee my affection,
my thoughts and my actions.
Let me be a pure nothingness
That Thy adorable Will be
Fulfilled, now and always.

To become "pure nothing" is foreign to a contemporary Western perspective. But to become pure nothing is an aim that is well-known in all the mystical traditions. It is one aspect of the *via negativa*, as it is called in Christian spirituality. By following the negative way we recognize our essential nothingness; this, however, is not worthlessness. Rather, our nothingness is simply a humble recognition of reality when viewed in relation to the totality that is God.

Jesuit writer William Johnston has explored the *via negativa* as he experienced it in Zen meditation. Sitting *zazen* in meditative practice aims at bringing the mind to a standstill. The ordinary thought processes—both words and images—are blocked, either by the meditator's efforts to be "nothing" or by confounding rational thoughts with an illogical problem or *koan*. In this way the conscious mind is divested of its images and its ordinary thinking capabilities. The mind remains in darkness, in emptiness. The value of "nothingness" is felt experientially. A sense of honest humility and deep peace tends to arise. Life's complexities are washed away and the meditator knows a deeper sense of what is truly important.

Murray Bowen, who was a family therapist, researcher, and theoretician, realized a similar mystical insight late in his life. When Bowen was invited to speak to family therapists and trainees who were trying to understand the intricacies of human dynamics, this master therapist would reiterate: "We are just sparks, like a flicker in the universe." When viewed with this attitude, all of our troubles and concerns are put into perspective. In the grand scheme of things how much does it really matter if Johnny gets into Harvard, or if Grandma goes on complaining? We are all merely sparks in the universe, just brief flickers of light.

Emptiness does not mean being irresponsible or unkind, but promotes a deeper way of living. As Thomas Merton discovered, universal compassion through emptiness is the essential aim of Buddhist meditative practice. These days many Westerners are drawn to Buddhist meditation, especially the Zen discipline. In *The Still Point*, William Johnston wrote about how the mind shifts during the process of meditation:

> Our thinking is an extremely complex matter. We do not just think on one layer of consciousness: for beneath the stream of thoughts and images flitting across the mind are other layers of consciousness, barely perceptible....We are not just thinking on one plane but on many planes simultaneously....The mind may be compared to a sea with many undercurrents, some of which may rise occasionally to the surface....In Zen...a new type of mental concentration sets in;...mind begins to work vigorously at another level. I have called this thinking "vertical," as opposed to the ordinary "horizontal" thinking when images are flitting across the mind. Thinking vertically, the stream of images halted, the mind goes down, down, down...the horizon of consciousness is extended, broadened, deepened....Going farther and farther down, one reaches a still point where peace reigns even while above there may be a storm.

So despite the churning waters that may be present in our consciousness, Zen meditators have found that there is a deeper place within us where peace and serenity reign. It is no wonder then, that Zen practice has such an appeal in our contemporary Western culture. Meditation is good for us, for the body and psyche as well as the spirit. Meditation can help us cope with pain, as Jon Kabat-Zinn has found in his clinics in Massachusetts. It also regulates blood pressure and lowers the risk of cardiac problems. Many behavioral medicine centers recommend various forms of meditation to help their clients reduce anxiety; meditation can help us cope with all sorts of difficulties.

Developing a meditative stance

There are many forms of meditation practiced by the world's spiritual traditions. What they all have in common is focused attention. For lay people, a set period of time is recommended for meditation, usually twenty to thirty minutes, preferably twice a day. Those living a monastic life, of course, spend much more time at it, sometimes even practicing meditation and contemplative prayer full-time for years on end.

The first step in meditation is to choose something on which to focus. This should be something simple: a flower, a painting, a lit candle, an icon, or a mental image. Auditory people may choose to focus on a piece of simple music, bird song, a gong, or the sound of ocean waves. One can also choose to use a mantra, a brief word or phrase repeated over and over. This latter form of meditation originated in India and the Far East but it has long been part of Christian meditative practice. We can use any sacred word or short phrase for a mantra, e.g,. Jesus; shalom; alleluia; Lord, have mercy; Divine Mother; your will be done; Abba, Mata; Allah; Om; and so forth. Brief phrases, perhaps ones that resonate with our own religious tradition, work well. Longer, formal prayers can also be used but a brief mantra is usually best to quiet the mind.

One meditation I particularly like is a three-part sequence that goes deeper with each step. To begin, focus on a mantra with a sacred name for about ten minutes. Next, shift the focus to a visual image such as a candle flame or soft light. Hold this for ten minutes as well, keeping the image in the center of the forehead, often called the "third eye." Finally, there is a deeper movement into the heart where the aim is total silence. I find it is easier to remain in this silence after having used verbal and imagistic phases to deepen my awareness and consciousness. To me, this process feels like going home—into my home of the heart.

The inner space of emptiness is the still point where peace reigns. I do not want to suggest that the path to this point is easy or a quick fix. Nor do I want to give the impression that I myself have gone the whole way. That would be hypocritical; few are the great masters who have traversed the deepest realms of the heart. But I do want to say that we can be students of the great masters and traverse the paths that they have followed.

In the West today, we are fortunate to be exposed to numerous spiritual teachers from the East. In any sizable city you can find Zen Buddhist centers or yoga classes with Hindu meditative practices. It is not unusual to find workshops in Kabbalah, from the Jewish tradition, and Sufism, from the Islamic tradition. Christianity too has come to an awakened interest in spiritual practices. The Trappist order of contemplative monks has been a seedbed for the renewal of Christian contemplative practice, particularly noted in the teachings of Thomas Keating and Basil Pennington. In *Thomas Merton, Brother Monk*, Pennington writes about Merton's contemplative search:

> Exposure to Eastern thought can be helpful in enabling us to break down the blocks in our thinking. [Thomas Merton] can help us here. Tom was well aware he was a Westerner and

that he wrote for a largely Western audience. He was deeply steeped in the Western Christian tradition. He was, indeed, a very traditional person. Yet he exposed himself as fully as he could in his circumstances to Eastern thought and practice. He was encouraged in this by masters such as Dr. Suzuki and excellent teachers such as Dr. Wu. And he did well. Some of the masters whom he met in Asia said that they had never met a Westerner who understood them so well. From the depths of his own tradition…he met them in the lived experience of their own tradition.…His understanding is deep and rich.

One cannot fully understand contemplative life unless one has lived it. Merton devoted long years to the search for God within his own soul. He understood the need to empty himself so that he could enter into his deepest center and pass through that inner place into an extraordinarily keen awareness of God. He wrote:

> The fact is, however, that if you descend into the depth of your spirit…and arrive somewhere near the center of what you are, you are confronted with the inescapable truth, at the very root of your existence, you are in constant and immediate and inescapable contact with the infinite power of God.

In the emptiness, we discover there is infinite fullness. Hayao Kawai agrees: at the ultimate point of complete emptiness, the awareness arises that emptiness and fullness are the same. But, he adds, you must discover this yourself. Although Buddhism is known as a nontheistic religion or philosophy, its practitioners still come to discover that at the center there is "something vast and unnameable."

By whatever name we call it, there is at the core of our very being a precious awareness of the presence of the divine. The

Trappist monks have developed a method of access to that inner place, called centering prayer, a name they chose because of the ways in which Thomas Merton articulated his own inner process. The following description is a rare personal account that Merton wrote to his friend, a Sufi scholar:

> Now you ask about my method of meditation. Strictly speaking I have a very simple way of prayer. It is centered entirely on attention to the presence of God and to His will and His love. That is to say that it is centered on *faith* by which alone we can know the presence of God. One might say this gives my meditation the character described by the prophet as "being before God as if you saw Him." Yet it does not mean imagining anything or conceiving a precise image of God, for to my mind this would be a kind of idolatry. On the contrary, it is a matter of adoring Him as all....
>
> There is in my heart this great thirst to recognize totally the nothingness of all that is not God. My prayer is then a kind of praise rising up out of the center of Nothingness and Silence. If I am still present "myself" I recognize that as an obstacle. If He wills He can then make the Nothingness into a total clarity. If He does not will, then the Nothingness actually seems to itself to be an object and remains an obstacle. Such is my ordinary way of prayer, or meditation. It is not "thinking about" anything, but a direct seeking of the Face of the Invisible, which cannot be found unless we become lost in Him who is Invisible.

In similar vein, the seventeenth-century Christian mystic Angelus Silesius talks of the emptiness that is required for a full contemplative awareness of God's presence: "God, whose love and joy are present everywhere, can't come to visit you unless you aren't there."

If we take these great mystics at their word, we can readily see that it is worthwhile to enter into our hearts and seek the emptiness there. Practically speaking, however, it is not always easy to empty our minds. We are habitually so busy with thoughts and images that, as beginners, we find it very difficult to still our minds. That is the essence of meditative practice.

All the meditative practices previously described will serve to quiet the mind. Each works to develop concentration and increase one's capacity to deepen awareness. Centering prayer is one practice that has been promoted in recent years by Basil Pennington and Thomas Keating. This practice generally begins with a contemplative reading of Scripture, called *lectio divina*. According to Pennington, one continues the meditative method as follows:

1. Sit quietly, in a relaxed pose. Bring your faith and love of God into your present awareness. Be in the silence, knowing that God is with you.

2. Take a sacred word or image—some reminder of how much you are loved and how much you love God. Gently bring that love word or image into your awareness. Whenever you become aware of your mind wandering, gently bring it back to center by using your love word or sacred image.

3. Continue in silence, in still awareness of the center of your being, using your sacred word or image to return to center whenever you stray.

4. End your period of centering with a formula prayer, perhaps the Lord's Prayer or the twenty-third psalm.

Though simple, the effects of this technique are profound. As Pennington writes: "Centering Prayer opens our hearts to God, cleanses the mind and soothes the soul."

You will recall the profound experience of Shelly, the contemplative woman in Chapter One who found that the eye of her heart was opened after several years of centering prayer. Many other individuals, laity as well as monastics, find centering prayer a tremendously rich experience. Sometimes its effects are therapeutic. At other times it may feel frustrating, with sessions seeming like "two minutes of prayer and twenty-eight minutes of spaghetti," according to Pennington. But regardless of the struggles or the dry periods, the deepening occurs.

In the next chapter we will look at some of the varied experiences we can expect as we make progress on the psychospiritual journey.

CHAPTER FIVE

A Spiritual Outlook

It is a misty morning in late August. The geraniums and impatiens are particularly beautiful against the gray sky and the deep green background of the woods. This has been a wet summer so the vegetation is particularly lush. And now, as Labor Day approaches, there is a special poignancy in the air. All of nature seems to know that summer will soon be over.

I sat this morning with my prayer group: six women who have been dialoguing and praying together for many years. Sometimes we sit in silence. Often we pray for the special needs of friends and family members, as well as for global concerns. Today we prayed for peace: what if each nation and each ethnic group put aside enmities and just let the others be? We prayed for the vast multitude of people who are ill or disabled, and for those caring for them. We also felt a personal sadness in the group today. As we each get older, there is a growing awareness that the winter of our lives is coming and we need to prepare ourselves for the harsh realities of illness, disability, and the end of life.

During our prayers we heard of one friend who has Parkinson's disease, and another who died of a sudden heart attack. We talked and prayed about our own fears: cancer, Alzheimer's, life in a wheelchair. One woman who was recently widowed talked about the burial of her husband; another talked about the cremation of her sister. Strange as it may seem, this conversation was not macabre but comforting. As most of us in the group are in our sixties, it is good to acknowledge and share our thoughts about moving into a new phase of life. Although the spectre of physical or mental deterioration is indeed fearsome, we are bolstered when we look at it as women of faith. We see our lives not only as winding down but also as moving ever closer to God.

Old age and death are part of the natural cycle of life. I saw this clearly in an Hasidic nursing home where I once worked. Every Tuesday all the elders who were mobile were brought to the activity room where they sat in a large circle. Inside the circle would be some young Hasidic mothers and their children. The babies and their mothers would simply sit and play, and occasionally a toddler would show some "great accomplishment" to the admiring elders. Here the cycle of life was complete: young children, adults, and elders. In that place I sensed we are all in God's hands, all perfectly lovable just as we are.

As I consider the fact that each day I am getting closer to the end of life, I feel some fear. I also feel some sadness in knowing how much I will have to let go; curiosity about what happens at the moment of death and what will happen after that; and hope that God will guide me so that I can go through the late stages of life gracefully with whatever pain and sorrow there may be. I hope I will feel God's presence with me through it all.

When Pierre Teilhard de Chardin was in midlife he too looked ahead to the end of his life. Out of the anguished awareness that life is transitory, Teilhard wrote an exquisite prayer which he called "Communion through Diminishment":

It was a joy to me, O God, in the midst of the struggle, to feel that in developing myself I was increasing the hold that you have upon me; it was a joy to me, too, under the inward thrust of life or amid the favorable play of events, to abandon myself to your providence. Now that I have found the joy of utilizing all forms of growth to make you, or let you, grow in me, grant that I may willingly consent to this last phase of communion in the course of which I shall possess you by diminishing in you.

After having perceived you as he who is "a greater myself," grant when my hour comes, that I may recognize you under the species of each alien or hostile force that seems bent upon destroying or uprooting me. When the signs of age begin to mark my body (and still more when they touch my mind); when the ill that is to diminish or carry me off strikes from without or is born within me; when the painful moment comes in which I suddenly awaken to the fact that I am ill or growing old; and above all at that last moment when I feel I am losing hold of myself and am absolutely passive within the hands of the great unknown forces that have formed me; in all those dark moments, O God, grant that I may understand that it is you (provided only my faith is strong enough) who are painfully parting the fibers of my being in order to penetrate to the very marrow of my substance and bear me away within yourself.

The more deeply and incurably the evil is encountered in my flesh, the more it will be you that I am harboring—you as a loving, active principle of purification and detachment. The more the future opens before me like some dizzy abyss or dark tunnel, the more confident I may be—if I venture forward on the strength of your word—of losing myself and surrendering myself in you, of being assimilated by your body, Jesus.

You are the irresistible and vivifying force, O Lord, and because yours is the energy, because of the two of us, you are infinitely the stronger, it is on you that falls the part of consuming me in the union that should weld us together. Vouchsafe, therefore, something more precious still than the grace for which all the faithful pray. It is not enough that I shall die while communicating. Teach me to treat my death as an act of communion.

What an act of faith it is to treat one's fatal illness not as an abhorrent invader that disturbs one's life, but rather as a messenger and agent that draws one to God! The angel of death is an angel of God. Can we learn to see the touch of that angel as a loving touch? One woman I know had a dream that ended with the words "*Death is the great purifier.*" What a gift it is to see that death need not be fearsome, but a significant and necessary process to prepare us to see God!

Teilhard was right when he wrote that we usually feel that "the future opens before me like some dizzy abyss or dark tunnel." Yet, in his faith, he realized that an entirely different viewpoint is possible. With grace, he hoped to attain a sense, not merely of acceptance, but of true transcendence. God, "the irresistible and vivifying force," is calling us home.

The eyes of a mystic can truly see all of life as infused with the divine. It is relatively easy to see God in the rocks on the beach, the moss in the garden, the mold in the basement, the birds calling from the treetops, the children at play. But can we also see the presence of God in the television stories of violence abroad or in our own country, or in conflicts within our families, within our religious or spiritual communities? How can we see God in all this misty, murky stuff of life?

Is God suffering with us? Is God in the middle of it all like one great therapist, working to help us live more lovingly together? (As a therapist myself, I rather like this god-image, although it is overly anthropomorphic.) These reflections brought to my mind a passage from a book by Carl Ernst, about the Sufi mystics of Islam. He writes that their belief system is based upon

> ...the names of God as the primary given from which extrapolations may be made. God's essence is forever unknowable and transcendent....[God's] names designate his attributes which are the intelligible aspects that constitute the world....
>
> The divine names can be divided into two classes, reflecting God's majesty (*jalal*) and beauty (*jamal*)....Underlying the division is the assumption that everything comes from God, both life and death, hardship and success...the conviction that God is responsible for everything in creation.

This is essentially a mystical outlook, one I share in the deepest core of my being. It is not popular these days to say that God may be part of sorrow, hardship, failure, and violence; yet we all know these are the realities of life.

In contrast to our Western viewpoint, the Sufis see all life infused with God. Similarly Hindus have no problem in seeing all of life in God's hands. To them God is a tripartite deity who is responsible not only for creating and maintaining life, but also for the destruction and ultimate recycling of all that lives. When we look to the cycles of nature, replete with falling leaves, decaying processes and renewal out of that very decay, the idea of the "destructiveness" of God does not seem so abhorrent.

Buddhists believe that all life is "perfect" just as it is. If we can come to recognize the suffering within and around us, then our task is not so much to do something to change things, but rather to be present even in the midst of suffering and be compassionate to those in need.

Common mystical aspects

There are many similarities when we look in some depth into the world's major spiritual traditions. I would like to identify here what seem to be those essential points of agreement. First, all the traditions emphasize worship and service. Then, at a deeper, more mystical level the traditions call their spiritual aspirants to a lifestyle that includes some form of *asceticism, silence, simplicity, surrender, prayer* and *meditation,* and openness to seeing the *sacred in the ordinary.* Let us look at some of these common mystical aspects.

Asceticism is the practice of living a simple and disciplined life in order to attain a higher spiritual state. This practice was very popular in medieval times, but is largely out of favor today. Nevertheless, there is a spiritual value to asceticism that is particularly important in our materialistic society. Rather than being complicit with the cultural voices that tell us we need more, more, more of everything, asceticism suggests that we place a cap on our desires and expectations. Curbing our instincts and taming our senses tends to reduce egocentricity, with its insistent thoughts of "I, me, and mine."

Asceticism need not be harsh. Rather, it can be a moderate form of renouncement. We can buy fewer things. We can gently say "no" to some of the demands of our bodies. People who follow twelve-step programs, for example, know that abstinence from harmful substances, including some foods, is not easy but can be both healthy and spiritually uplifting. Saying "no" or "not yet" to the greedy child within and curbing our desire for instant gratification can further spiritual growth. These are choices we can make in our everyday lives, ones that can bring about deep happiness and peace of mind.

Sometimes asceticism is beyond our choosing. When we become ill or aged and infirm, we often cannot control the bodily processes. We do have a choice, however, in how we accept our natural physical decline. Graceful acceptance is a spiritual attitude. Letting go of desires allows new forms of spiritual appreciation and gratitude to emerge.

I recall one cold wintry day when I was working in the Hasidic nursing home. It was a caring place—a sacred space in many ways—but despite the commitment of the staff, most of the elderly residents wished they were not confined there. Most missed their freedom. Many of the residents tended to isolate themselves and, as often happens in nursing homes, the staff would try to draw them into activities of one sort or another. This particular winter day I was looking for Miriam, a resident who was on my visitation schedule. I found her sitting in her wheelchair by the back door, looking out the glass door to the winter scene outside. Seeing her sitting alone, some on the staff might readily have wheeled her back to get her involved in some art project or musical activity. Instead I pulled up a chair and watched with her for a while before starting to speak.

Miriam was looking at the beautiful snow-covered trees just outside the door. In that narrow strip of doorway Miriam had gained a view of the world that was deep and precious and personal. "It's beautiful"—that was all she said for a while. I was moved almost to tears by the simplicity and the silence, and her sense of wonder. I felt her remarkable ability to find the sacred in an ordinary view of snow on evergreens. This doorway was her sacred space, her place of peace. Here she found joy.

As we talked later on, I learned that Miriam had come to accept her placement in the nursing home. She was not depressed or even lonely, although she did value the time we had to talk together. Here was a mystic, an ordinary woman who found delight in the God to whom she had surrendered her fate.

We all have a need for *silence* in our lives. With the high-stimulus environment of our Western culture, many people are starved for quiet. They deeply need the soul-refreshing waters of silence. They want to recharge their batteries, to let go of their stress. They want time to pray, to meditate, to reflect on their lives, and to commune with nature. They want an interlude where they can be contemplative.

Others—often young people, if they are unaccustomed to silence—may feel anxious about being quiet for a time. Their resistance to silence is similar to what we may encounter in the initial stages of any new venture, a foreboding about what we will find in an unfamiliar situation. Yet moving into silence is often a surrender in itself. We ask ourselves questions such as, What does God have in store for me? Can I trust God? Can I trust this process? Am I too unworthy to benefit from this? In silence, issues of self-esteem tend to surface. If we can let ourselves be in the silence, however, profound changes may ensue.

Out of the silence a desire for *simplicity* often arises. The Quakers, for whom silence is an important part of their worship, give a good example of a lifestyle marked by simplicity. They well know that God speaks to us in the silence of the heart. Simplicity is also seen in the natural lines of both Scandinavian and Shaker furniture, or of Japanese gardens and flower arrangements. The art of Zen is simplicity itself, natural beauty, a lack of pomp, ornamentation, and fussiness. Simplicity and silence go well together, and encourage a contemplative approach to life.

Mystic consciousness is available to us whether we are relaxing, enjoying the beauty of nature, or in a busy city environment. Contemplation is a way of being that is not in opposition to action; rather, it is a different attitude with which we can approach life.

As we wake up each morning, do we take up the reins and the

control of our lives? Or do we say to ourselves, as the mystics do, "I wonder what God and I are going to accomplish today?" In the pale light of dawn each day we can *surrender* to the divine and remind ourselves that we are merely instruments of the creativity of God. If we are willing to be God's hands and feet then we have taken on a little of the flavor of mystical surrender.

I once had the opportunity to have breakfast with Antoine Feuvre, a French scholar of the European mystical tradition. He was explaining the heart of the mystical quest, and he said to me, "Read Jacob Boehme! That's the essence." According to Feuvre, Boehme understood that surrender to the divine will is the key to the mystical life.

Following this lead, I learned that Boehme was a seventeenth-century German mystic who was very influential on the later English mystics. He was a simple man, known as "the shoemaker of Gorlitz." Nonetheless he was eloquent and passionate in his desire to know and follow God's will. In a book called *The Way to Christ*, he wrote:

> O God, Holy Spirit, my Savior…teach me what I ought to do so that I might turn to You. Redirect my will in me to You….Enlighten my spirit so that I may see the divine way, and continually walk in it. Take me from myself and give me completely to Yourself alone. Do not let me begin, will, think nor do anything without You.

Boehme further wrote: "There is a revelation of the hiddenness of God in all being and life." The mystic is one who can see God in all things. He or she quite naturally sees the *sacred in the ordinary*—not just in the flight of the bird or the dance of the leaves; not just in the beautiful but also in the ugly.

Where is the sacred in the graffiti on city walls, or amid the litter, or in the lives of people bowed down by poverty? Where is the sacred behind prison walls? Where was the sacred at Auschwitz? Elie Wiesel, a mystic of profound sensitivity, could see it there. Where is the sacred in Hollywood hullabaloo? James Hillman appreciates the sacred in the ordinary, even there.

I believe there is a mystic consciousness that resides within each one of us. If we look for the sacred in the ordinary, we may find incredible beauty in the people who surround us. We then become gift-givers, and bring to others an awareness of their own beauty. We mirror the extraordinary sacredness we see in them.

The religious and spiritual traditions of the world vary tremendously in what they consider appropriate or effective ways of communicating with the divine: from African drumming to Baroque organ music, from the sweet tunes of flute or harp or chimes to the utter simplicity of human breath, from human voices chanting to a full choir singing Handel. Even the attentive ear can celebrate the Creator in bird song or the crashing waves at the seashore. Sound reverberates with heartfelt prayer, whether prayers of petition or prayers of praise and gratitude.

Meditation differs from prayer in that it is often wordless and highly concentrated. Focus is on a single point—a repetitive sound, constant image or bodily process (heartbeat, breath, or repetitive motion). Meditation can carry one deep into the interior of one's own being wherein an experience of the sacred is received. Committed meditators, practicing one-half to one hour a day, find an ever-deeper experience that is extraordinarily peaceful and self-reinforcing. Knowledge of this inner space is what has motivated mystics throughout the ages. Then, ideally, the fruits of prayer and meditation are brought into ordinary life.

In the next chapter we will discuss the fruits of such practice as it affects our personalities and our daily lives.

CHAPTER SIX

Healing Our Wounds

The Dalai Lama is one of today's spiritual masters who teach the importance of compassion and loving one's enemies. In a 1981 talk at Harvard University he remarked on the similarity of great religious figures and on their willingness to suffer for others:

> For me it has great significance that the way of life of Buddha, Jesus Christ, and other past teachers is marked by simplicity and devotion to the practical benefit of others. All of these leaders supremely exemplify in their behavior voluntary assumption of suffering—without consideration of hardship—in order to bring about the welfare of other persons....As followers of these faiths, we must make sure to consider this essential similarity.

Embedded in Buddhism is the idea of the *Bodhisattva*, one who, after reaching the highest realms of enlightenment, renounces the opportunity for *Nirvana* in order to return to life as a helper for humankind. Compassion is the essence of such a life. In comparison, the Judeo-Christian-Islamic traditions emphasize the importance of charity and compassion in this life in order to please God or to save one's own soul, as well as to help one's neighbor.

As the Dalai Lama said, many of the great spiritual teachers, including Jesus and Buddha, call us to a life of "simplicity and devotion to the practical benefit of others." Yet often, such a way of life is not practiced by the followers of these religious masters. What stands in the way? How can the spiritual path help heal the wounds that lead to these obstacles?

From my own experience, both personal and professional, I have come to the conclusion that meditative practice can be very helpful in healing our wounds. This comes about in two ways. First, the heightened concentration in all meditative practices brings issues to the surface of our consciousness. This can be healing in and of itself. As Gestalt therapist Fritz Perls used to say: "Awareness heals." Second, meditation gives us a deep sense of being totally accepted and loved by God. We will look at this aspect of meditation later on in this chapter.

Psychologists who practice in the Buddhist tradition have studied the parallels between meditation and psychotherapy. In his brilliant book, *thoughts without a thinker*, psychiatrist Mark Epstein writes about the psychodynamics of meditation:

> The most moving experiences in meditation are those that enable the meditator to come face-to-face with various cherished images of Self, only to reveal how ultimately lacking such images are.
>
> Much of what happens through meditation is therapeutic, in that it promotes the usual therapeutic goals of integration, humility, stability, and self-awareness. Yet there is something in the scope of Buddhist meditation that reaches beyond therapy, toward a farther horizon of self-understanding… meditation takes actual qualities of mind and cultivates them internally so that the person's powers of observation are increased. With these increased contemplative powers, the meditator is then able to scan and to hold what can be

described as the building blocks of self-experience, the basic cravings that give rise to the sense of self. In so doing, one's deeply ingrained sense of self is profoundly and irrevocably transformed.

Mathew was a young Catholic priest who had been practicing Buddhist-style breath meditation for about fifteen years. When he came to me in psychotherapy I could sense immediately that he was earnest, intense, and quite wounded. Mathew was easily angered and anything that seemed to him hierarchical would set him off; he felt put down when anyone else was considered to be superior to him. Needless to say he found life in the Catholic Church difficult.

Whereas he enjoyed the adulation of his parishioners—he was an effective, popular priest—he would also cringe whenever he was criticized. Not only was he distressed when his bishop corrected him, but he was also easily angered when lay people on the parish council disagreed with him. Fortunately, Mathew was blessed with a contagious laugh and a ready wit so his parishioners forgave him for his bouts of petulance. They did not realize how easily he felt humiliated by any suggestion that he was a less-than-perfect priest.

Mathew was particularly bothered by a problem that he rarely spoke of. He felt a great deal of inward competitiveness in relation to others who were following a spiritual path. With his dual affiliations, he had met both Catholics and Buddhists who were spiritual seekers. He confided in me that he felt threatened when he encountered people who seemed to have greater spiritual attainment than himself.

During our work together, Mathew revealed that he had come from an affluent home but seldom felt appreciated there. He never felt that he was loved for being himself, only for the ways he could make his parents feel proud. He was sent to private schools where he learned that academic excellence was a ready route to affirmation from both his teachers and parents, affirmation that he sorely needed. Mathew succeeded in school, and went on to a highly-rated university, but he was left with a secret "hole in the soul," where he felt unloved and basically unlovable.

Once the therapeutic issues were on the table, we began to look at how Mathew's spirituality was helping him to cope, and how it might be beneficial in helping him to heal. He said that the Buddhist practice of mindfulness was particularly helpful to him. When he remembered to be present in the here and now, he could see how his anger was triggered whenever he felt humiliated. Further, he could see that these feelings of humiliation originated in his own mind; that is, it usually was not something that the other party intended.

During a long Buddhist retreat, Mathew dedicated himself to focusing on the rhythm of his breath as well as on what his mind was doing whenever he lost his meditative focus. He gained real insight that weekend, and he came back to therapy elated. He told me, "I realized, for the first time, that my feelings of humiliation are illusory. I don't have to feel 'put down,' even when others criticize me. If it bothers me it's because I let it bother me. I'm not really as worthless as I sometimes feel!"

Then Mathew switched into his Christian consciousness and said: "Even though my parents probably didn't give me enough attention or affirmation for just being me, I realize that God loves me just as I am! I've preached it many times, but this weekend I know I really felt it: God loves me, Mathew, just as I am, imperfect as I am. It's OK with God that I'm just me." I smiled, feeling delighted with the insights Mathew had received during his meditation retreat. I knew that no one could have told him what he had just found out. He had to discover it for himself.

In my own psychospiritual growth and development, I find the combination of working with dreams and practicing meditative awareness during the day to be most helpful. I use the technique recommended by many of the spiritual traditions—Christian, Sufi, Hindu—that is, repeating the name of God or some other short mantra or sacred phrase as often as possible. I have not yet come to a place where I pray continually but that is my aim, and sometimes I sense I am coming closer to that way of being.

Many years ago, I was present at a talk given by the Christian contemplative Brother David Stendl-Rast. The title of the talk was startling: "How to Pray an Apple." Brother David said many helpful things that day, but what stands out in my mind is how he told us that eating an apple can be an act of worship. Eat the apple with full awareness, he said, present in the moment and offering gratitude for the blessing of the good taste and nourishment.

I did not realize it at the time, but I am sure Brother David had been exposed to the Buddhist practice of mindfulness. To be fully present, awake, and aware is a mindful way to eat an apple—or to do anything else in life. As some Buddhists say: "Mindfulness means to do what you do when you're doing it." To be in the present moment and to recognize it as a gift from God is an outlook that reverberates in the Judaic-Christian-Islamic traditions, as well. As I have said before, at the contemplative, mystical level, there is really no essential conflict among the various religious traditions. Each has different techniques that can be helpful in bringing us closer to God.

Buddhist masters teach that when we meditate, the mind will jump around like a monkey. This "monkey mind" is not totally random, however. What tends to come up into our consciousness is all sorts of unfinished business that vies for our attention. To the Buddhist practitioner, these bits of cognition or images—whether related to the past or future—are simply to be brushed aside, gently bringing the mind back to the here and now, and to the meditative focus. Western psychotherapists, however, have found that when we stay with the practice of here-and-now awareness we find both the sources and the solutions to our mental pain. I have noticed that solutions often have to do with accepting our imperfections and essential fallibility in light of God's complex universe.

The false self

As we read in Chapter Two, the false self is a phrase used by Thomas Keating to describe the facade we create of the perfect person we would like to be. It is the defense against our narcissistic wounding in childhood. Often it is many layers deep. The false self always wants to look good. It judges us and it judges others. It puts up walls of separation and erects defenses to protect us from criticism, rejection, and humiliation. All sorts of envy and competitiveness are encapsulated here. While we may be very proficient at looking good on the surface, we know at the core that such behavior is not authentic.

One aspect of false self that we find particularly among religious folks is spiritual pride. Although it usually is not present in our conscious awareness, at least in the beginning, spiritual pride often motivates even the most earnest of spiritual seekers. Mathew felt it: he needed to feel he was "more spiritual" than others. That is part of what led him to the priesthood in the first place, and what led him into Buddhist meditation as well. He needed to feel superior to others on the spiritual plane, even if he felt inadequate in other ways.

Horrible feelings of envy are another way the false self may manifest. In his beautiful book, *Invitation to Love*, Thomas Keating writes that "my early years in monastic community brought me face to face with the not-so-pleasant parts of myself, as I came to experience the false self in action." This was the most difficult part of Keating's struggle to become contemplative. He was dismayed to discover feelings of envy lodged deeply in his soul. At the same time, he became aware that he was in a process of purification which "usually begins when one enters a life of strict silence, solitude, and prayer: one's mixed motivation emerges into clear awareness. Grace is there, but so is the false self. The truth about ourselves is inevitable; whatever it is, it is going to come up….The great struggle is not to get discouraged when the divine reassurances recede."

Keating found that the person he most envied at the monastery turned out to be a blessing in disguise. When he could talk openly with the other monk, he found out that he too was having struggles with self-esteem and feelings of inadequacy, especially in terms of prayer. Keating began to realize that the troublesome people in our lives offer an opportunity to work on ourselves. They too are gifts from God. Keating wrote:

> In religious circles there is a cliché that describes the divine purification as "a battering from without and a boring from within." God goes after our accumulated junk…and starts digging through our defense mechanisms, revealing the secret corners that hide the unacceptable parts of ourselves….It is an invitation to a new depth of relationship with God. A lot of emptying and healing has to take place if we are to be responsive to the sublime communications of God. The full transmission of divine life cannot come through and be fully heard if the static of the false self is too loud.…Purification of the unconscious is an important part of the journey….

Psychotherapy in real depth can be enormously helpful in working through self-esteem issues, and many clergy and monastics avail themselves of the opportunity to clear out what Keating calls "the garbage" in their own psyches. We need to realize that the process of psychospiritual growth is never-ending. God continues to work on us in many ways, both cleaning out the internal "junk" in our psyches as well as creating and gratifying the aspiration that calls us into deeper spiritual states of being. Keating wrote:

> The experience of God's love and the experience of our weakness are correlative. These are two poles that God works with as he gradually frees us from immature ways of relating….The experience of our desperate need for God's healing is the measure in which we experience his infinite mercy. The deeper the experience of God's mercy, the more compassion we will have for others.

I have had such cleansing experiences myself, usually at a time when I am ready and praying for personal growth. For instance, after long years of my own depth psychotherapy, I thought I had worked through all the major issues and core problems in my psyche. But then one night, seemingly out of the blue, I had a horrible nightmare. *In the dream there was a murderous madwoman— totally irrational. She was murdering her children and anyone else who got in her way. Envy was her driving force, and it turned out that she was inordinately envious of anyone who had a nicer house than she did. She was an archetype of furious envy, like Kali, the malevolent Hindu goddess, in her most destructive power.*

I was stunned by the dream, realizing immediately that this madwoman was a previously undiscovered part of myself. At that time, I was preparing to lead a workshop and was a bit anxious about "looking good" as I knew some of my highly-esteemed colleagues would be present. I had prayed for help and guidance.

Needless to say, I was appalled to discover such rage and envy operative within me, but the awareness allowed me to work with the issue consciously rather than let it smolder internally.

That day, I asked God to heal the dark space within my psyche that had just been revealed. I went on to teach the workshop feeling truly humble. I was no longer concerned about being "the best" workshop leader. Rather, I was aware that I was every bit as wounded as the participants I would be teaching. Quite clearly, I felt a sense that we were all in this together.

If we truly want to make progress in the spiritual journey toward God, then we need to expect there will be times when we are confronted by our abject spiritual poverty. The picture may not be pretty, but the self-knowledge it brings is extraordinarily valuable.

Feelings of inferiority or superiority, like envy, are significant clues that we are dealing with the terrain of woundedness and the false self. They may point to what some psychologists call the "impostor syndrome." This is the fear that we will be found out as being inadequate. It is a deep-rooted, terrible fear of not measuring up. No matter what evidence there may be to the contrary, we fear we are simply not good enough. "Sooner or later," we surmise, "I will be exposed as an impostor."

Unconditional acceptance

The second aspect of healing that occurs in the psychospiritual journey is the recognition of being loved by God. Divine love is ultimately the greatest healer. As Thomas Keating said: "Once we start the spiritual journey, God is totally on our side. Everything works together for our good." When our practice of mindfulness and awareness makes us conscious of what we are doing and where we are going, healing begins to flow directly from our relationship with the divine. Here is where we might say the angel of the heart moves in to teach us that we are loved.

Do we really believe that God is love and that God loves us unconditionally? Many of us were brought up with fierce images of God. These were usually engendered by well-meaning people who feared that we would not behave well unless we had the fear of God (or the fear of hell) drilled into us. Unfortunately, that kind of fear does not tend to foster mature believers who can understand and relate to God as love. It is commonly accepted that children learn better when they are supported and affirmed. Likewise, we relate better with God when we are in touch with the loving, merciful aspects of the Divine One.

Among the Sufi mystics, a favorite practice is *dhikr*, meaning "remembrance." This is achieved through recitation of one of the ninety-nine names of God, among which are a wide range of attributes. Those who use this practice in their prayer can choose the name that is most meaningful to them at any given time while they traverse the psychospiritual path. The wisdom of the Sufi masters reminds us, however, that we need to focus first and foremost on the loving, merciful aspects of the Divine One; only later are we capable of looking at the complex issues related to justice and authority in a world that includes suffering.

Thomas Keating points out that there are many stages in our development as believers and persons of faith. In *Invitation to Love*, he writes of four key stages where we are asked to consent to an ever-deepening awareness of our relationship with the divine: "In childhood, God asks us to consent to the basic goodness of our nature with all its parts." This means that, even as children, we need to recognize we are just the way God created us, and that all creation—including ourselves—is good.

Keating goes on: "In early adolescence, God asks us to accept the full development of our being by activating our talents and creative energies." The emphasis here is on developing ourselves to be all we can be within the context of moral responsibility. We say "yes" to God by choosing to actualize our potential to the best of our abilities, given the circumstances of our lives. This continues through young adulthood, when we learn how to live authentically and begin the task of dismantling the false self. We have many opportunities and challenges to develop ourselves as people who are able to love well and serve others through our work. It is a time when we learn that we can use our loving, sexual energies as a motivating force "to serve other people with affection and warmth," as Keating put it.

By midlife we often find that the stability of our adulthood begins to shift. New avenues open up to us and we are drawn inward, as well as outward, to new ways of being. One big aspect of this shift, often called the midlife crisis, is due to our growing awareness of life's finitude. Our limitations are before us, no longer easily denied. Keating describes this as the time when "God invites us to make a third consent: to accept the fact of our non-being and the diminutions of self that occur through illness, old age, and death." This is a potent reflection to make. Tomás Agosin used to say, "When you have fully looked at death in the face, what other response can there be but to celebrate life!"

Finally Keating hints at the ultimate consent, the surrender to God and the willingness to be drawn into union with the divine. As he describes it:

> The fourth consent is the consent to be transformed. We might think that everybody would be eager to make this one, but even the holiest people are inclined to say, "Let's not rush into this!" The transforming union requires consent to the death of the false self, and the false self is the only self we know....Some of us are more afraid of the death of the false

self than of physical death.

These four consents are invitations to welcome life and death as God's graced gifts and to appreciate the vocation of being a member of the human family in this marvelous universe with all its beauty and potentialities.

So here again we are confronted with that potent, often terrifying concept of surrender of the ego—or, as Keating calls it, the false self. The Sufis use the term "annihilation"; for them, it is a central part of their spiritual journey from start to finish. To be in union with God, as the mystics realize, is to let go of the sense of separateness.

Sufi master Ibn 'Arabi has written an inspired retreat manual in which he portrays the whole mystical journey through meditative, contemplative stages. Towards the end of the journey, what is revealed to the mystic is the heart of the process of creation: the "Pen" that writes the marvels of the universe and then the "Mover of the Pen," that is, God. But even here, he says, the journey is not quite complete. The mystic is still separate, still an observer of the processes of God's creative power. Then comes the ultimate annihilation when one is ready to make that final surrender.

Ibn 'Arabi writes: "And if you do not stop with this, you are eradicated, then withdrawn, then effaced, then crushed, then obliterated." This is not an experience that most of us are likely to welcome. We tend to agree with Thomas Keating's way of putting it: "Let's not rush into this!" Yet we know this ultimate surrender is essential for progression into the full state of union with the divine. One of the most famous of the Christian mystics, John of the Cross, called this experience "the dark night of the soul." It is the ultimate surrender, when our whole self is let go. This ultimate surrender is only possible, it seems, if one has practiced smaller surrenders along the way.

The contemporary Indian holy man Sri Sathya Sai Baba also teaches about the meaning of divine union and the importance of letting go. We begin, he says, by detaching from our individual, selfish desires. We let go of our materialism by placing a cap on our desires and tame our egos by putting a ceiling on our ambitions. This is the practice of asceticism, which is a gentle way of reminding us that God is central and in control of our lives.

"But, but, but," I hear you say, "it's healthy to have a desire for the good things in life." This is true, but only up to a point. Sooner or later, if we are to make genuine, significant progress in the psychospiritual journey, we will have to renounce our desires. We must let go and let God.

Surrender is an essential aspect of all the mystical traditions, whether of the East or West. Although renouncing our desires seems almost unpatriotic in our materialistic modern culture, nevertheless we need to understand the value of desirelessness. For that understanding, it is helpful to turn to the East, where its true meaning has not been lost.

CHAPTER SEVEN

A Look to the East

The roots of the great banyan tree surround me as I sit in the cool shade on a hill overlooking Puttaparthi, a small town in southern India. This is known as the Meditation Tree. Years ago, Sri Sathya Sai Baba buried a metal plate, capable of producing intense vibrations, next to this tree in order to make meditation deep and pure. I feel the vibrations in my legs as I sit, looking at the mountains in the distance, listening to bird songs and drumming from the ashram down the hillside below. This is a sacred space. Here I sense God's presence in myriad ways.

Ewert Cousins, mystical theologian and leader in interreligious dialogue, has noted that the banyan is a vast and symbolic tree, one that speaks to many primal peoples at an archetypal level. From its branches new roots descend to the earth, each forming a new tree that remains connected to the mother-tree in elemental ways. I think of this as representative of the many world religions, all of which surround, descend from, and remain connected to an essential mother-tree. As Cousins writes:

> At this point of history, because of the shift from divergence to convergence, the forces of planetization are bringing about an unprecedented complexification of consciousness through the convergence of cultures and religions....the reli-

gions must meet each other in center to center unions....in which differences are valued as a basis for creativity....

This global consciousness, complexified through the meeting of cultures and religions...is global in another sense: namely, in rediscovering its roots in the earth....We must rediscover the dimensions of consciousness of the spirituality of the primal peoples....We must recapture the unity of tribal consciousness by seeing humanity as a single tribe...related organically to the total cosmos.

For many years I have had a deep desire to travel to India. I did not want to see the Taj Mahal and other great palaces and temples, as much as to experience the intense spirit of this profound and ancient culture. Also, having lived most of my life in a green, affluent suburb in southern Connecticut, I could only imagine what life is like in a parched, impoverished region in rural India. I wanted to know the reality of a Third World country, and pictures from *National Geographic* cannot suffice. I felt the need to know, firsthand, that humanity is a single tribe, even as we celebrate our diversity.

When a friend told me about a conference to be held in Delhi called "Education for Global Unity," I was given the impetus to make the trip I had been longing for. This opportunity seemed like a gift from God, and I began to make immediate plans for the trip. Even the events of September 11, 2001, which frightened many Americans away from flying and prompted the cancellation of the Delhi conference, did not deter me. By then, I was emotionally ready to make the journey alone, halfway around the world, to visit this land of ancient spiritual traditions.

Once in India, I came to Prashanti Nilayam, the Abode of Highest Peace, which is the home and ashram of Sai Baba, to spend a thirty-day retreat spanning Christmas and the New Year.

For me, this is a time of immersion in Indian culture. Words seem simply inadequate to express the impact India has had on me. This is the land of the Vedas, 6000-year-old scriptures, with a living tradition that is deeply mystical and centered on continual worship. There is a universal, spiritual ambiance here, amid the exotic sights, sounds, smells, and flavors characteristic of Indian culture.

Being present, here and now, brings to me a sense of sacred beauty beyond compare. The architecture of Prashanti Nilayam is typical of Hindu temples. The building has many-tiered towers and sculptures in soft blue, pink, and cream. When seen in the early morning sunrise, with the mountains in the background, the structure fits perfectly with its surroundings.

The countryside around the ashram is much like the southwest United States, dry and desert-like, with fabulous rock outcroppings. I had expected to see poverty and primitive conditions in this rural area, but the unexpected beauty of the rickshaws and oxcarts, the little shacks and hand-painted decorations on everything surprised and filled me with delight right from the start.

Then there is the beauty of the people and their extraordinary spiritual devotion, beyond anything I could have imagined. For me, the physical beauty of the women in saris is surpassed only by the beauty in the eyes of the children. But above all is the beauty of spirit—their *bhakti*, or devotion to God—that can be observed everywhere: roadside shrines decorated with flower garlands that are changed each day; the sound of chanting with incredible power and vibration; throngs of people arising at 3:30 a.m. in order to worship in their most sacred places; mandalas painted anew on the doorsteps each day; sun-worshippers standing with arms upraised at dawn to greet the sun. The spiritual energies of India are truly palpable. The Spirit of God is very much alive in the Indian people!

I have been profoundly moved by the love and peace I find here in this ashram. Before arriving, I was not at all sure of what I was getting myself into. I quickly discovered that an ashram is something like a huge retreat house. Living quarters are dormitory-style, and I sleep in a room with seven other women from as many different countries around the world. Communication with each other is through sign language and broken English. A typical day starts early, with a cold shower (there is no hot water). Then there is time for meditation, manual work (usually serving meals or drying hundreds of metal plates afterwards), lectures, and communal singing. Several times each day, we sit to receive *darshan*, or the opportunity to see and experience the presence of Sai Baba.

Who is Sai Baba? To his devotees he is an *avatar*, or manifestation of the divine. There are thousands of miracle stories that involve Sai Baba, and I have witnessed the results of many of them. The interested reader can find many accounts of his life and works in the volumes listed in the resource section of this book; here I will simply describe him in terms of what I have directly perceived.

Each day, while thousands of devotees wait breathlessly to see him, this little man appears like a dot of orange as his robe is seen in the distance. As he comes closer one can see his dark skin and bushy, Afro-style hair. Now in his mid-seventies, he looks like an old man: barefoot, slightly rounded shoulders, a slow gait. But I, like others who sit with him day after day, have felt the subtle vibrations of his energy, and I have seen the rays and aura of his light. I have seen his loving attention as he receives the letters devotees present to him, and I personally have experienced his loving smile, his wave, and his hand raised in blessing. His voice is loud and clear, and he speaks with authority when he teaches, giving his discourses in the Telegu language, which is then translated into English.

Sai Baba is not a haughty man. He lives simply and gives of himself tirelessly. There is no sign of egotism in him; for a powerful world leader with thirty million followers worldwide, that is a miracle in itself. Sai Baba models selfless service, teaching simply: "My life is my message. Love all, serve all." He is a charismatic spiritual leader who has accomplished great good, both within individual hearts and minds, and at the societal level, building free hospitals, schools, and dams that provide safe water for hundreds of towns around.

Sai Baba is truly universal in his outlook and reveres all the world religions. "A religion that does not teach how to respect other religions is no religion at all," he writes. There is a great *stupa* in the garden outside his residence, a column erected to the five major world religions: Judaism, Christianity, Islam, Hinduism, and Buddhism. Flags of these religions decorate the walkways, and art objects depicting Jesus of Nazareth, Buddha, Moses, and Mother Teresa of Calcutta dot the landscape along with shrines and statues of the traditional Hindu deities. In this ashram one feels great love for all people, no matter what their beliefs.

Multitudes of visitors come to the ashram from nearly every country in the world. The message here is cosmic, and the universal qualities fostered are *sathya* (truth), *dharma* (righteous living), *shanti* (peace), *ahimsa* (nonviolence), and *prema* (love). Although Sai Baba's teaching echoes the Vedas, the ancient Indian scriptures, and the Bhagavad Gita, he frequently emphasizes the similarities in the scriptures of all religions. His mission is primarily to teach humans to find the divine life within each of us. This Self, or Atman, is the central core of his message: God is love. Find love within you.

Hindu understanding of the divine

As we listen deeply to the Vedic scriptures, with Sai Baba as our translator, we return now to the ideas and practices that foster the universal spiritual quest. We will travel farther along the mystical path, again touching on the ideas about surrender, then moving beyond, toward the mystical meaning of union with the divine. As background, let us look first at the ancient Indian perspective on surrender and unity.

In India the concept of God is more complex than that of Western religions. Basically there is reverence for both the transcendent deity (what we call God the Creator and the Hindus call Brahman), and the immanent deity (our sense of Holy Spirit, which is quite close to what they call Atman). For the Hindu, Atman and Brahman are one. God is within each human being, fully and completely immanent in each of us, as well as transcendent to all of life. "That thou art" (*Tat Twam Asi*) is a familiar Hindu saying that emphasizes this basic identity. This concept does not mean different gods, however. Rather, it recognizes the essential unity and presence of divinity in all of us.

Sai Baba echoes the Sufis and the Christian mystics when he talks about the advanced states of spiritual growth. In conversation with an American, Dr. John Hislop, he revealed there is a state where "there is no body and no mind....This is Divine consciousness where God alone is." Sai Baba also clarified a point about the meaning of surrender. He said: "The word 'surrender,' in English, is not quite correct, it is not the right word....When you say, 'surrender,' you are separate and God is separate....But God is not separate." Here Sai Baba was expressing the traditional Hindu, Vedantic idea of non-dualism: God is all there is.

Before looking at some of the Indian spiritual teachings and exploring their value for Western spirituality, it would be helpful to have some background in the Hindu tradition. In the book *Hinduism and Christianity*, Swami Satprakashananda gives a comparative understanding:

In approaching the teachings of a religion other than one's

own, it is not only easier but more enlightening to consider the similarities rather than the differences. The background of Christianity, like Hinduism, is Asiatic. Both religions believe in the Incarnation of God in human form. And in the teachings of both religions, devotion to God, and His grace and love in return, are particularly stressed.

From the standpoint of Vedanta, the teachings of all the great spiritual leaders of the world are revered and accepted as pathways to the one Supreme God. Jesus Christ, like Sri Krishna and the Buddha, is regarded among the greatest human manifestations of divinity. His life and teachings exemplify truths which are indispensable to anyone who is devoted to the search for God.

This universal outlook is generally accepted among Hindus. They are very broadminded in their theology and comprehensive in their approach to spirituality. In the Hindu tradition there are four general, well-known spiritual paths or ways to meet God. They are the paths of knowledge (*jnana*), good works (*karma*), intense meditative practice (*raja*), and loving devotion (*bhakti*). The highest mystics are considered to be those for whom all four paths are united.

It has been frequently stated that the easiest, most generally successful path in our current era is *bhakti*. In one of his earliest teachings, Sai Baba said:

> The Lord is a mountain of *Prema* (Love); any number of ants carrying away particles of sweetness cannot exhaust His Plenty. He is an Ocean of Mercy without a limiting shore. *Bhakti* (devotion) is the easiest way to win His Grace and also to realize that He pervades everything; in fact, is everything! *Sharanaagathi* (total surrender), leaving everything to His Will, is the highest form of *Bhakti* (devotion).

In a similar vein, the Bhagavad Gita, a central ancient text that has generated repeated commentaries throughout the ages, places spiritual wisdom in the mouth of Krishna, an *avatar* who disguises himself as a charioteer for the warrior prince, Arjuna. In Krishna's key teaching on selfless action, he explains that karma yoga is a way of living more effectively and happily. The secret, he relates, is in living a God-directed life. This is the way to be spiritual while fully active in the world. Do your best, he tells Arjuna but don't get "caught" in the world. When you surrender the ego, you become "selfless" and you live only as an instrument of God. This is the secret also of union with God! This text tells us too that when we live as instruments of God, nothing is ever wasted; never are we failures. In Jack Hawley's recent, very readable translation of the Gita, we hear Krishna saying:

> Arjuna, those who have found the pure contentment, satisfaction and peace of the *Atman* (the True Self Within) are fulfilled....The point, old friend—and this is very important—is to do your worldly duty, but do it without any attachment to it or desire for its fruits. Keep your mind always on the Divine (*Atman*, the Self). Make it as automatic as your breath or heartbeat. This is the way to reach the supreme goal, which is to merge into God.

Krishna also seems to be saying here, "stay focused." Keep an unwavering mind, focused on union with God and on doing God's will. This will avoid the uncertainty of a quavering mind that gets pulled in a thousand directions. To accomplish this kind of inner transformation, we have to remember to let go of our desire for personal reward, to let go of our desire for pleasure and power. These are selfish desires and they block the utter concentration we need for union with God.

To accomplish this aim, we need to focus on going beyond all our natural inclinations and all our worldly attachments. Concentrate, Krishna tells us, on being free from the "tyranny of the pairs of opposites": good and bad, lovable and hateful, pleasant and painful. To get trapped in the apparent opposites is a "common debilitating malady." Carl Jung agrees; he was probably influenced by the Bhagavad Gita when he theorized that true Self is found at the point of intersection of all the pairs of opposites.

In the Gita we hear Krishna speaking from the perspective of God, telling us to remain calm and centered in the Atman. He further teaches us that we should avoid seeking acclaim and acquiring earthly possessions. A similar theme is found in the Isavasyopanishad, as commented upon by Sai Baba:

> All things of this world, the transitory, the evanescent, are enveloped by the Lord who is the real Reality of each. Therefore, they have to be used with reverent renunciation, without covetousness or greed, for they belong to the Lord and not to any one person....The Universe is the Immanence of the Lord, His Form, His body....The Universe...is the same as He....Work without the desire for the fruit thereof slowly cleanses impurities like the crucible of the goldsmith.

Sai Baba's teachings frequently center on the theme of unity. As in all theistic mystical traditions around the world, he believes that the ultimate aim of the spiritual life is union with the divine. Occasionally Sai Baba teaches about the more advanced spiritual states, including a "super-consciousness" in which the devotee experiences a state that is beyond recognition of body and mind. Visions may be present in that state. He says, "In the super-conscious state there is still a very slight tinge of duality, of giver and receiver." But, he teaches, "There is still a state beyond the super-conscious." He calls this ultimate state divine consciousness. He continues, "In divine consciousness there is the giver only. Really, all other than the One is false....This is Divine consciousness where God alone is." Here we see the essence of mysticism: such complete union with the divine that there is no longer any differentiation. Giver, gift, and receiver are all one.

According to Sai Baba, the Atman resides in every heart. He emphasizes that God is love, and that we are to relate to one another from the center of love that lies within each and every one of us. In his conversations with Dr. John Hislop, Sai Baba said:

> Even in persons of unpleasant nature, be aware that the Lord is in the heart even of that person. Have that aspect in mind and treat the person from that viewpoint to the best of your ability. In time that person will respond and his nature will change. One sees people as good or bad because he does not see the person in full, but only one-sided.

Then Dr. Hislop asked: "How does one see God Himself?" and Sai Baba replied: "In order to see the moon, does one need a torch? It is by the light of the moon that one sees the moon. In like fashion, if one wishes to see God, it is by love, which is the light of God, that one may see Him."

By the light of love, people the world over are seeking to find the divine. Perhaps if we understand that universal search, and if we have greater empathy for the many ways in which God is revealed, we will be less likely to fall into territoriality, superiority, and general isolation that prevents us from seeing our essential unity as children of God.

I would not presume to define who the Atman might be for you, or how God may work in you. Rather I would say, as they do in India, "*Namaste*," meaning "The God in me greets the God in you."

At the ashram, I wrote this in my journal: "I pray for all of you who will read this work. May your spiritual practices be deepened, purified, and strengthened." As I completed those words, I dedicated this book to all who will read it and I asked for Sai Baba's blessing on each one.

On the last Sunday of December, at the end of morning darshan, Sai Baba passed where I was sitting. I raised the first draft manuscript of this book to him with a whispered prayer: "Please." He came over, looked at the first page and reached out his hand. The manuscript, then tentatively entitled *The Angel of the Heart*, was personally touched and blessed by the hand of Bhagavan Sri Sathya Sai Baba on December 30, 2001, at Prashanti Nilayam, Puttaparthi, India.

CHAPTER EIGHT

All Is God

We are at a time in history where a paradigm shift is occurring as we move from strictly linear thinking to an appreciation of the complexity and interrelatedness of systems. This shift is occurring in our experience of God as well! For many people, our god-images today are no longer simple and easily defined. Years of theological explication have fleshed out what each tradition believes, but we are now at a time when the traditions themselves are recognizing the similarities as well as differences among them.

As I have studied and talked with colleagues in the field of psychology and religion I have come to realize that not only are we a world uniting with a need to understand multiple traditions, but also that we are all unique individuals developing spiritually within complex global networks.

The Christian monk Thomas Merton understood both the universality of God's manifestation in the world and the uniqueness with which we each perceive God. He knew that there is profound religious experience in calling God by name. In this, Merton, the Sufis, and Sai Baba would all agree that the most profound form of meditation is to repeatedly call God by name. Merton wrote:

Each person knows God by a special name....Each one

speaks to God with a name that he alone has for God, and God speaks to him with a name God has for him....The secret of the life of prayer is to find the name of your Lord...and to speak to Him who is your Lord. Don't speak to someone else's God....One has to be careful not to impose on other people one's own Lord, your own idea of God....To have this name of God by which we know Him, by which he makes himself known to us, is to receive...God's mercy.

While we are all formed within the bosom of our native religious traditions, at some point we are exposed to varied approaches to the divine which often serve to enhance our faith life. More importantly, we all have unique experiences wherein we get glimpses of how God is being made manifest to us as individual spiritual beings. Recently, I asked a group of Protestant clergy how they image God today compared to the god-images they had in childhood. Their responses were revealing. Several said they used to image God as an old man with a beard; medieval iconography has no doubt influenced this childhood image for many Christians.

One man said he imaged God as a great eye in the sky. That was the image painted on the dome of the church he attended as a child. He said, "I was always afraid, and I was sure that he would see every fault and mistake, as well as every sin I made." Another man, who was a Jewish psychiatrist, told me that when he was a child, his nanny brought him to her Catholic church. There he saw a huge crucifix with Jesus, who was obviously suffering on the cross. This child knew that Jesus was Jewish, and it made him afraid. He wondered about how this Jewish Jesus could be made to suffer so much.

Other childhood god-images are kindly in nature. Adult Christians often remember the image of Jesus as good shepherd, or the famous picture of Jesus knocking at the door, waiting for the faithful to open it. Many people admit they were most impressed by the Christmas scene where Mary played such an important role. Now that they are adults, a feminine component to the god-image often takes the foreground. This is especially true for feminists, and increasingly we find individuals who worship God as "Divine Mother."

Today many adults have a more amorphous god-image: a cloud, a force, or the energy of the universe, for example. This type of thinking is in line with Buddhism, which sees emptiness or something vast and unnameable as the center of all existence. Jesuits who have been influenced by Zen Buddhism, such as William Johnston and Robert E. Kennedy, ask questions like "What is the 'still point' within the soul?" Thomas Merton also ponders the "point-vierge, the center of our nothingness where, in apparent despair, one meets God—and is found completely in His mercy." And in India, Sai Baba has written: "The form of God [is] energy.…Everything is a temporary form of energy and is suffused with it."

Certainly God is far beyond anything we can conceptualize; we are tremendously limited in our ability to conceive of or image God. We might hold to the *via negativa*, where God is identified as "not this, not that," cutting away all misconceptions until the absolute nothingness is found, or to the *via positiva*, where complete fullness is thought to be the ultimate personification of God. As for myself, I think there is one God who is known by many names, and that no visual image can begin to capture the reality that is God.

Ibn 'Arabi's approach to the problem of how to conceptualize God is instructive. Drawing on his mystical experiences, he described five levels or planes in which the manifestations of God can be found, with each plane becoming increasingly concrete. First is the Unmanifest, the Source of all being. From this Divine Source all else emerges. Second is the plane of the various gods or names of God, e.g., Allah for the Muslims; Yahweh, Elohim, Adonai in the Jewish tradition; Siva, Vishnu, Durga, Kali in the Hindu tradition; the Great Spirit of the Native Americans; and so forth.

At the third plane there is "the Lord," or the ways in which God manifests or incarnates more concretely in our perceptible reality. Jesus and the *avatars* of India would be examples of this level of the divine being. It should be noted here that a basic tenet of Christianity is the unique position of Jesus as Son of God. Other religions, such as Hinduism, accept the sonship and incarnation of Jesus but question the uniqueness of that position.

At the fourth plane lies all humanity. Here, says Ibn 'Arabi, one can find God's presence in each and every human creature. Finally, at the fifth plane, lies the rest of creation. The dolphins and the planets, the trees and rocks, the brilliant fall leaves, the blue sky, and even creatures as small as a gnat, all these are manifestations of the divine. There is a great Oneness of Being.

The mystical insight here is that all is God. Ultimately, says Ibn 'Arabi, all beings return to the Source. So, from this perspective, there is a progression of manifestations of Divine Being until the ultimate return, as each eventually reunites with the Source. One reason I like this conceptualization is that there is no room for an everlasting hell; each creature has potential for conversion. Each will return to God. Every creature, no matter whether we might judge it "bad" or "good" by our human standards, is in its "latent essence" a manifestation of the Divine Oneness of Being.

When I talk with friends and spiritual companions about these ideas from a Sufi mystic, I often have to remind them that very similar ideas can be found among the Christian and Jewish mystics. Julian of Norwich expressed a sense of wonder as she held a small hazelnut in her hand; Francis of Assisi is well known for his tremendous respect for the Godlife in all creatures. In Judaism we find the story of the great Rebbe Bal Shem Tov, who laced his boots with such reverence that it was a profound spiritual experience simply to watch him. He too found the presence of God all around him.

While reading about Ibn 'Arabi's outlook on the Oneness of Being, I came across a passage that he wrote about the heliotrope, a plant that behaves almost prayerfully, worshipping the sun as it moves across the sky. Shortly after I read this, with this idea of the prayer of the heliotrope still in my consciousness, I met for prayer with my small group of Christian women. It was a lovely summer day so we met outside on a patio surrounded by trees. After our meeting, I sat for a while in the sun, still in a prayerful mood. The theophany I perceived in that moment was a small glimpse of how God is revealed in all of nature, and I recorded my experience in the following words:

My Lord, you reveal yourself to me,
To you and through you.
In the quiet summer morning I bask in the sunlight,
While friends talk and plan their lives
A million miles away.
I am with the pines, the birds, the butterflies, the sunshine.
Suddenly I see You
In the gossamer aura encircling the sun.
Spider web of huge and perfect proportions
Exquisitely placed, centered on the sun.
What heliotrope creature created such a web?
What amazing Creator
Creates anew this gifted sight today?
Even the pine needles encircle the sun,

An act of worship that calls to my deepest Self.
Praise be to you, my Lord!
My heart swells in gratitude
To know the goodness
Of your peace.
Amen.

From the infinite to the infinitesimal, all life that surrounds us is God's Self-revelation. The mysteries of the vast cosmos—from the solar systems all the way down to the workings of insect colonies, bacteria, viruses, genetic codes, atoms and beyond, to realms that science has not yet begun to conceptualize—are truly awesome. All this is manifestation of the divine. So too is human nature, with all its idiosyncrasies, patterns, and systems—all this is God being made manifest to us in myriad ways.

Seeing God in suffering and infirmity

I am sitting in the sun at a Franciscan retreat house on a beautiful fall day. In the distance I hear a large group of retreatants. They are from Alcoholics Anonymous, and they are working on the "fourth step" in their recovery from alcoholism. I know God is with them. I agree with Ibn 'Arabi, that God is found even in the midst of adversity, including alcoholism and the struggle towards honesty, responsibility, abstinence, and recovery. Today these retreatants call on their Higher Power—the name by which they identify the divine—to help them in their recovery. Each step of the way is a step in God.

Can we honor God in every aspect of life? It is easy to see God manifest in my sweet little granddaughter, for example; but it is much more challenging to find God's manifestation in the genetic disorder that caused the death of her twin brother at nineteen months of age. To see illness or disabilities as sacred is not easy.

Yet that is what the saints and mystics have taught us to do. Teilhard de Chardin's wisdom regarding life's "diminishments" is profound. Aging, illness, death—can we abandon ourselves to God's providence as Teilhard does? Can we pray, as he did, "when the ill that is to diminish me or carry me off strikes from without or is born within me…when I feel I am…absolutely passive within the hands of the great unknown…O God, grant that I may understand that it is You"?

Another way to look at infirmity comes from the East. It is well-known that Prince Gautama, who came to be known as the Buddha, was startled into his spiritual sensitivity by his first unexpected confrontation with illness, old age, and death. What was he to make of this? The pampered, sheltered young prince was aghast to see ugliness and suffering beyond anything he could ever have imagined. When he learned that all people die, he could no longer avoid the issue. And so he set forth on his own to find the cause of such suffering.

As he sat under the Bodhi tree, after years of ascetic privation, the Buddha waited for the insights that would help him to understand human suffering. What he realized, quite suddenly, was that all life is suffering and humiliation; that the cause of suffering lies in our attachments; and that to extinguish suffering, one must let go of the natural attachments we all carry with us. These were profound insights. Buddha coupled these "Noble Truths," as he called them, with a way of life centered on compassion. These insights and the way of compassion continue to be central to Buddhist thought and practice today.

What Buddha was finding is that suffering is not pain itself, but rather the psychological way we relate to pain. Buddhist practitioner Stephen Levine works extensively with patients who are dying. In *Who Dies: An Investigation of Conscious Living and*

Conscious Dying, Levine gives us precious glimpses of a way to go through the most difficult passages of our life, more with a state of interest—even reverence—than with fear and suffering.

Levine writes of the awareness needed to die with grace. Whether we have two days, two months, two years, or twenty years left in our lives, the work is the same: to live fully and consciously, accepting the whole of our being, not shunning or denying any aspect of our life experiences. In his intimate work with dying patients, Levine came to realize that death forces us to pay acute attention to what is going on. Thus, whether in meditation or in the actual dying process, focusing on death is a way of becoming fully alive. Our attention, our awareness is what produces the feeling of liveliness, and a sense of peace and support. As Levine writes:

> That is where our experience of life arises….The more attention, the more alive we feel. Perhaps that is why so many who are dying also say that they have never felt so alive….Perhaps the first recognition in the process of acknowledging, opening, and letting go that we call "conscious dying" is when we begin to see that we are not the body. That consciousness is constantly in a process of unfolding. We see that we have a body but it is not who we are….
>
> One fellow remarked that he could see that he was "creation constantly in the act of becoming." He saw the perfect unfolding of each moment and that there was nothing he had to *do* about it, that all his doing to *become* something or someone just "dulled the wonder of it all."

In this process of conscious living—or conscious dying—what we must do is the important spiritual work of detachment. Not only do we detach from our body, but we also let go of all our other ego identifications, the sense of "this is who I am." We disattach from our natural desire to have things the way we want them to be—or the way we think they ought to be. That means not getting uptight and angry when we feel cheated financially, when we feel that others are trying to manipulate or control us, when we feel disrespected, or in other adverse circumstances of life. It means letting go of our habitual roles, as well as of our materialism and possessiveness.

Detachment also means letting go of our great admiration for youth and beauty. I personally find Michelangelo's statue of an old woman a wonderful reminder that there is beauty of all sorts in every stage of life. Letting go of what we treasured in the past means disattaching from those we love when changing circumstances require it: our children, our friends, our spouses and lovers. These too are passing; or as Buddha would say, all life is impermanence.

I remember the profound sense of loss felt by so many patients in the stroke unit of a hospital where I once worked, when they found their capacities suddenly limited. Some could not speak; some could not walk. Many felt they had been "sentenced" abruptly to life in a wheelchair. They often felt fear, sorrow, and anger at the seeming unfairness of their fate. They needed to grieve and recall the many aspects of life as they had experienced it as mobile, communicative adults. Then, most importantly, they had to let go of all that. They needed to recognize that, somehow, they now had to find a new sense of meaning and purpose—a new sense of richness—in their changed circumstances.

Living consciously means being aware of life around us and within us at this very moment. As I sit today in the sun, seeing brilliant orange maple leaves against a crisp blue sky, it is easy to feel God's presence. I see the shiny gossamer of a spider's thread, and I can peacefully recall the God-sent gift of the heliotrope spider web that so moved me last summer. But now other retreatants have come outside and I am disturbed by their talking. Yet I must remember that this too is of God. Then silence returns, and I am grateful. The sound of a bell, birds chirping in the trees, leaves rustling as the wind blows them. Talk is in the distance now, the sound of cars very distant. I recall what Sai Baba once said: "For those who are attuned, all sound is the sound of the great Om," the sacred syllable that literally means "all." In this statement, Sai Baba is echoing what Ibn 'Arabi believed: all of life is the Divine One being made manifest.

Life is such a treasure. When we are fully aware, the blessings of life seem to come bubbling to the surface. When we let go of the moments that have passed and focus on the present rather than our worries about the future, then we are free to notice the little blessings of each day.

As I sit at the retreat house, I am aware of the white butterfly flitting past my foot; the bumblebee gathering its nectar from a lavender aster; the middle-aged man in dark green shirt who kisses a tree and then teaches two women to pray with the tree, feeling their energy grounded even as the tree is rooted in the earth; the sound of an airplane in the distance, held up in the sky by science and technology. These moments cause me to marvel.

We spend so much of our time complaining, gossiping, or criticizing ourselves and others. If we knew that this would be our last day on earth, would we waste our time this way? I think not. I think our thoughts on our last day might run more readily to an appreciation of what we would be losing. We would be unlikely to let that last day go by as insignificant.

Each moment in our lives is precious; each moment is of God. Our gift is this very moment. It is our very own theophany.

Surrender into life; surrender into death

Mysticism for our postmodern age is, in many ways, like the mysticism of the past. Yet there are differences as well. The mystics of the past followed the angel of the heart, learning to love God in emptiness or fullness, each according to the religious tradition of his or her own heritage.

There are many role models of past times who can lead us toward sanctity. For example, John of the Cross, the great seventeenth-century Spanish mystic, inspires us by the power of his love when he writes:

> Sometimes my heart is so full that I feel as if there were a burning flame of love within me, so strong that it could consume my whole being. How can I contain these fires of Love? How can I seek moderation in my desire for God?

So too, Hafiz, the fourteenth-century Sufi mystic, writes with the same intensity:

> Love is the Great Work.
> Though every heart is first an Apprentice….
> Happiness is the Great Work
> Though every hardship first becomes
> A student to one who really knows
> About Love.

In the present era, we can still be inspired by such mystic poetry. It seems, however, that we are being drawn further, not only to deepen our spiritual life within our own traditions but also to learn how to transcend the specifics of religious tradition in order to find a wider church, a more extensive temple, a mysticism of the all-encompassing heart.

Theologian Hans Küng has said that we will not have peace until the religions understand one another, and that we will not have understanding until we have in-depth dialogue. If this is true then it seems to me that the peace we all so ardently desire requires a broadening of our perspectives into the mystical domain. We are at a time in history when we must move beyond arguing whether god-images should be male or female. We are, in fact, at a radical turning point where world religions emerge as a unitive force. Are we being called by the Universal Deity to discover the similarities that underlie the mystical traditions?

To find a universal spirituality we must, first of all, be willing to surrender our preconceptions and beliefs that "our way" is the "right way." There is truth to be found in each of the traditions; of that I am convinced. We must be willing to let go of our sense of superiority and our emphasis on differences in order to find the value of crosscultural similarities. Moreover, we must treasure the differences. As Mike Bastia, the Native American spiritual leader, said, "If we look into the natural world we see that the Creator loved to have diversity."

Where do we find unity in the midst of diversity? I think we have to surrender our rational theologies in order to move beyond conceptual thought into the realm of mystical experience. The mystics have all told us that we cannot think our way into unity. We have to surrender the intellectual process, and with it, the insistence of our ego that it has the "right answer" to every question.

When we surrender and accept the death of our ego, we move into a realm of unknowing. In this realm trust is essential. For those with a theistic background, this plays out as trust in God—however we name the divine presence. For those in nontheistic traditions, trust may be more amorphous: trust in the Tao, in the undefined flow of life, in the formless infinite, or simply in the vastness.

In my own search for a unifying image for the divine source of all life, I find the image of Divine Mother to be especially resonant. I think of all the great goddesses who have been worshiped in various cultures, especially in pagan times. Then I think of

Mary, Mother of Jesus, the most powerful and beloved of the saints in the Catholic tradition.

Many of the great shrines to Mary in Europe, as well as in South and Central America, were built upon sites that were originally dedicated to the pagan goddesses. This was brought home to me during a trip some time ago, to Assisi in Italy. There I sat one early morning on the fifteenth of August, the feast of the Assumption of the Blessed Virgin Mary, waiting on the steps of the church for the Mass to begin. As I waited, I meditated on the Divine Mother and asked her to guide me in choosing a path to take at that point in my life. The image that spontaneously arose from meditation was one of monks in procession. I realized I was being called to begin a more contemplative phase of my life.

I felt that this call came directly from the Divine Mother. You may wonder, "Who was She who did the calling?" Was it the Blessed Mother of the Catholic tradition? Indeed, I was meditating outside her church, and in the courtyard was a statue of Mary standing on the moon. But I came to find out that on this site there once had stood a temple to the goddess Minerva. The worn steps and the great stone columns still echoed the history of this Roman goddess of wisdom.

Who is the Divine Mother? Is she "God," "goddess" or simply "the Mother of God"? I am not sure it matters; and I am quite sure we cannot figure this out with our rational minds. The answer, it seems, must be known experientially or it will not be known at all.

On another trip I had the opportunity to make a pilgrimage to one of the great Black Madonnas of Europe. I was visiting Zurich for a Jung conference, and we made a side trip up into the mountains, to the tiny town of Eiseldyn where the Madonna was housed. Before leaving, a small group of us prayed:

Let us follow God.

Let us walk in peace.

May the Unmanifest be made manifest,
even as the Manifest becomes hidden and
is made unmanifest again.

As our train began its Alpine ascent, we left behind the prim-
roses of the valley and entered a blizzard that coated the forested
mountainside with white. I thought of the history of this particular statue. She was made of wood and stood only about four feet
high. Because she was believed to be a powerful purveyor of miracles, this statue was once the object of warfare and pillage. She
was carried several hundred miles into the mountains to escape
enemy troops during a long-ago war. Was it through such mountain storms as we were now traveling that her saintly rescuer carried her? Then, history tells us, she was buried for a long period
of time; that is when the statue turned black. When she was
unearthed, in her blackened state, she was found to have a
greater-than-ever power to grant healing and other miracles.

There is a huge baroque church built to house the Black
Madonna at Eiseldyn. She stands at the back of the church, in the
midst of opulent artwork with gold clouds billowing out behind
her. In true baroque style, the statue is dressed in an ornate robe
of brocade and gold trimmings. Yet the dark wood of her face and
the infant Christ she holds are utterly simple and sweet.

That day, I sat in a meditative state before this Black Madonna,
gazing at her simple beauty. I held these questions in my heart:
"Who is Divine Mother? Will she, the unmanifest one, make herself
manifest to me?" As I sat gazing at the statue of the Black Madonna
for about half an hour, she showed me her many faces. Her coun-
tenance changed from female to male and back again. She changed
into many different images of persons throughout history: knights

and ladies, monks and nuns, peasants and rulers, modern scientists and ancient artisans. It is hard to describe the great sense of giftedness I received in her presence. The myriad qualities of the Divine One were revealing themselves to me. It was a numinous experience of the manifested divinity present in all beings.

When we let go of our individual differences and truly surrender our lives, we find the Divine One made manifest to us in great richness and beauty. The ordinary loveliness of nature and the extraordinary images that may emerge from our dreams and our meditative moments—all these are evidence of the great fullness with which life is enriched.

Union with the divine

What does union with the divine mean to the spiritual seeker of our own day? We know that in preparation, there must be purification of the soul, and a surrender of the individual will to the divine will. We know there are glimpses of illumination along the path. But what of mystical union? How can we begin to envision what lies before us when we choose the mystical path? I will attempt to put together a few tentative glimpses as I have understood them from readings of contemporary mystics, as well as those who are well along the psychospiritual path.

Union with the divine requires an inner wholeness where one's authentic Self is at peace with the various components of one's personality. The dark as well as the light side of the inner Self must be consciously in balance. This is the inner marriage or conjunctio, as Carl Jung understood it. But I am convinced that there is more than just inner wholeness.

The external conjunctio is where the individual soul must come to peace with the rest of humanity. As Jesus said, we cannot claim to love God and hate our neighbor. We must learn how to relate lovingly to the people we encounter in our daily lives. We must have concern, compassion, and charitable action for those who are in need in the world. We must place our lives on the line in some way to benefit the needy ones in the world.

Jorge Waxemberg is a contemporary spiritual leader from South America. In his book *The Art of Living in Relationship*, he writes that the mystical quest involves relationship on a number of levels: within ourselves, with our families and neighbors, with the whole of humanity, and with the cosmos. Each of these levels of relationship is critical to our quest for union with the divine.

One might wonder: "How do I relate to all of humanity, the millions of people I don't even know?" A key to this level of unity is found in the word "participation." First we must realize that everything we do affects all others. We are so interrelated that not one single action, not one single thought, goes by without affecting the whole. This is where network thinking comes in, when we become increasingly aware of the connections among us. When I buy a shirt, for example, I might think of all the people whose lives were involved in providing me with that garment—the farmers who sowed and harvested cotton, the weavers and seamstresses, the shop foremen and truck drivers, the salespersons and marketing managers. Whenever I do a simple act such as purchasing an item at a store or on the Internet, I participate in the work of all those people, whether I am aware of it or not.

The Internet is a good instrument to help us realize how very interrelated we all are. Whenever there is a slowdown we can be aware that there are millions of other people using the system at the very same time. Rather than be annoyed at the frustration of having to wait, we can take those few moments to say a brief prayer for all those people who are, at that very moment, interconnected by the wonders of technology. (I have found that this outlook helps immensely when caught in a traffic jam, as well.)

We can use this compassionate approach to network thinking in many ways. For example, if we have pain of any sort, we can use that experience to connect mentally with all others in the world who are experiencing pain at that very moment. Or when we have a moment of beauty we can mentally share that moment with millions of others who need a moment of beauty in their lives. We can see a sunset and realize that every day, all around the world, people are gifted with the beauty of clouds and sunlight. There are so very many ways we can intentionally think about our lives as intimately connected with all others.

Jorge Waxemberg, in his exquisite little book *Living Consciously*, writes about the participatory mindset involved in discovering "mysticism in our lives":

> Mysticism gives the mystic a sense of the eternal, and this consciousness helps one to overcome the temptation to live for today without responsibility for the future. The future is not only one's future but the future of all humanity....From the mystical point of view, everything that we do, as well as the way we do it, must lead toward an ever-increasing understanding of oneself, the world, and life. Everything we think and do must lead to a deeper and more far-reaching participation with the world that we know. Not only that, our participation must extend to a greater whole, a reality that is beyond our present understanding and comprehension, but which includes each one of us and the world that we perceive.

In regard to the mystical unity of all humanity, we cannot help but be impressed by the grand vision of Pierre Teilhard de Chardin. Teilhard was a Jesuit, a scientist, and a mystic. As a paleontologist he studied the rocks and artifacts of civilizations long ago. He came to realize that the earth has evolved by a process of unification and complexification. Single cells unite to form a human body, for example. Then the cells diversify and specialize so that all the functions of a human being are attained. This is a very high order of evolution, and it has taken millions of years to achieve.

What Teilhard realized—and this is a mystical insight expressed by his scientific mind—is that the next stage of evolution is the unification of the whole of the human species. He called this the "Omega Point," and he predicted that it would occur as the result of a shell of intellect, which he referred to as the "noosphere," that would surround the earth. Teilhard died on Easter Sunday in 1955, just a few years short of the first practical applications of the information technology that has created the World Wide Web, a shell of intellect or information that circles and encompasses the earth, just as he predicted.

Teilhard's grand vision is helping in the difficult task of uniting humanity. Teilhard said that the force of love will complete the process. It seems to me that, as we go deeper into globalization, we can cooperate or we can resist. When we lovingly attempt to understand and respect one another, we are furthering the process of global unification.

Today, increasingly, we are seeing the image of our earth—the blue planet—as symbolic of our essential unity. We are being called to love one another even as we love our earth. When we work together to save our planet from our self-imposed destruction, we realize there are many boundaries to cross in order to be effective. Rich and poor, male and female, business person and farmer, children and their parents from every nation: we are all in this together. As Jesus taught, we must learn to love one another, even our "enemies." We must find a way to act in consort, in cooperation, to save our common home. As we strive in countless ways for the welfare of all humanity, we are also furthering the cause of the divine will.

Union with the divine is still an elusive state. Not many of us have reached even the foothills of that resplendent mountain where rapture marks the attainment and reception of extraordinary grace. I sense, however, that enormous benefit can be gained by heading clearly in that direction. Can we orient ourselves toward mystical unity and trust the angel of the heart, the Holy Spirit, to guide us as far as we are meant to go?

The yearning is crucial. If we ask God to teach us to love (as Tom Wells suggested), and if we open ourselves to the various ways that God answers that prayer, then bit-by-bit our love will increase. All mystics yearn for union; nothing short of complete union will ever fully satisfy them. The mystics are lovers of God. Never do they take God for granted, but they continue to set their hearts on the ultimate spiritual aspiration.

Ultimately we must ask ourselves:

Can we open our hearts in yearning for God, even as God yearns for us?

Do *we* dare to aspire to mystical union?

Could we ever be fully satisfied with anything less?

Sai Baba and Ibn 'Arabi both tell us, from vastly different cultures and time periods, that in fact we *are* united with the divine. As the Hindus say, "That thou art." Perhaps a major step in coming into fully actualized union with the divine is the recognition that, *de facto*, we are already united!

To follow Sai Baba's account of the process, there comes a stage when the union is like a marriage. The Lover and the Beloved are fully in a state of love and gratitude. In the mystical marriage there still remains the duality of Giver and receiver. But beyond that there is only the One; duality evaporates. Our unique individuality is annihilated. All that remains is God consciousness.

Giver and receiver are One.

Bibliography &
Suggested Resources

Agosin, R. Tomás. "Forgiveness: Psychological and Spiritual Dimensions." *Seeds of Unfolding: Spiritual Ideas of Daily Living.* Volume VIII, 1991.

Baker, Rob and Gray Henry, eds. *Merton and Sufism: The Untold Story.* Louisville, KY: Fons Vitae, 1999.

Bashiruddin, Zeba. *Sai Baba and the Quranic Myths.* Prashanthi Nilayam, India: Sri Sathya Sai Institute of Higher Learning, 2000.

Bastia, Mike. *The Spiritual Journey: Interfaith Perspectives*, produced by Galen Films. New York: Auburn Theological Seminary and The Temple of Understanding, 2000, videocassette.

The Bhagavad Gita: A Walkthrough for Westerners. Trans. Jack Hawley. Novato, CA: New World Library, 2001.

Boehme, Jacob. *The Way to Christ.* Trans. P. Erb. Mahwah, NJ: Paulist Press, 1978.

Bosnak, Robert. *A Little Course in Dreams: A Basic Handbook in Jungian Dreamwork.* Boston: Shambhala. 1988.

Chittick, William C. *The Self-Disclosure of God: Principles of Ibn al-'Arabi's Cosmology.* Albany, NY: SUNY Press, 1998.

Collins, John E. *Mysticism and the New Paradigm Psychology.* Savage, MD: Rowman and Littlefield, 1991.

Corbin, Henry. *Alone with the Alone: Creative Imagination in the Sufism of Ibn 'Arabi.* Princeton, NJ: Bollingen, 1969.

Cousins, Ewert H. *Christ for the 21st Century*. Rockport, MA: Element, 1992.

———. "States of Consciousness: Charting the Mystical Path." In F. R.Halligan and J.J. Shea, eds. *The Fires of Desire: Erotic Energies and the Spiritual Quest*. New York: Crossroad, 1992.

de Chardin, Pierre Teilhard. *The Divine Milieu*. Trans. B. Wall. New York: Harper and Row, 1968.

Defillippis, Leonardo. *John of the Cross*. Harrison, NY: Ignatian Press, 1997, videocassette.

Epstein, Mark. *thoughts without a thinker*. New York: Basic Books, 1995.

Ernst, Carl W. *The Shambhala Guide to Sufism*. Boston: Shambhala, 1997.

Gibran, Kahlil. *The Prophet*. New York: Alfred A. Knopf, 1973.

Gyatso, Tenzin, His Holiness the Dalai Lama of Tibet. *The Dalai Lama at Harvard*. Trans. J. Hopkins. Ithaca, NY: Snow Lion Publications, 1988.

Hafiz. *The Gift*. Trans. D. Ladinsky. New York: Penguin, 1999.

Halligan, Fredrica R. *The Art of Coping*. New York: Crossroad, 1995.

Hislop, John S. *Conversations with Sathya Sai Baba*. San Diego, CA: Birth Day Publishing Co., 1978.

Ibn al-'Arabi. *The Bezels of Wisdom*; The Classics of Western Spirituality series. Mahwah, NJ: Paulist Press, 1980.

———. *Journey to the Lord of Power*. Rochester, VT: Inner Traditions International, 1989.

Izutsu, Toshihiko. *Sufism and Taoism: A Comparative Study of Key Philosophical Concepts*. Los Angeles: University of California, 1983.

Johnston, William. *The Still Point: Reflections on Zen and Christian Mysticism*. New York: Fordham University Press, 1987.

Keating, Thomas. *Invitation to Love: The Way of Christian Contemplation.* New York: Continuum, 1995.

Kasturi, N. *The Life of Bhagavan Sri Sathya Sai Baba,* 3rd ed. Prashanti Nilayam, India: Sri Sathya Sai Books and Publications Trust, 1986.

Kennedy, Robert E. *Zen Spirit, Christian Spirit: The Place of Zen in Christian Life.* New York: Continuum, 1997.

Krystal, Phyllis. *Sai Baba: The Ultimate Experience.* York Beach, ME: Samuel Weiser, 1994.

Levine, Stephen. *Who Dies? An Investigation of Conscious Living and Conscious Dying.* New York: Anchor/Doubleday, 1982.

Mercer, John. *The Journey of the Heart.* San Francisco: Muhyiddin Ibn 'Arabi Society, 1996.

Merton, Thomas. *The Asian Journal of Thomas Merton.* New York: New Directions, 1975.

Miller, Alice. *The Drama of the Gifted Child: The Search for the True Self.* Trans. Ruth Ward. (Originally published in Germany as *Prisoners of Childhood.*) New York: Basic Books, 1981.

Mitchell, Stephen, ed. *The Enlightened Heart: An Anthology of Sacred Poetry.* New York: Harper and Row, 1989.

Murphat, Howard. *Sai Baba, Man of Miracles.* York Beach, ME: Samuel Weiser, 1973.

Pennington, M.Basil. *Centered Living: The Way of Centering Prayer.* Liguori, MO: Liguori Triumph Press, 1999.

———. *Thomas Merton, Brother Monk.* San Francisco: Harper and Row, 1987.

Sai Baba. *Sathya Sai Speaks: Discourses of Sri Sathya Sai Baba,* Vol.1. Prashanthi Nilayam, India: Sri Sathya Sai Books and Publications Trust, 1953-60.

———. *Sathya Sai's thought for the day.* Prashanthi Nilayam,

India: Sri Sathya Sai Books and Publications Trust.

————. *Teachings of Sri Sathya Sai Baba*. Tustin, CA: Sathya Sai Book Center, 1974

————. *Upanishad Vahini: Writings on the Upanishads by Bhagavan Sri Sathya Sai Baba*. Bangalore, India: Sri Sathya Sai Publication and Education Foundation, 1999.

Sandweiss, Samuel H. *Sai Baba, the Holy Man and the Psychiatrist*. San Diego: Birth Day Publishing Co., 1975.

Sanford, John. *Dreams, God's Forgotten Language*. New York: Harper and Row, 1989.

Satprakashananda, Swami. *Hinduism and Christianity*. St Louis: Vedanta Society, 1975.

Stein, Murray. *Jung's Map of the Soul: An Introduction*. Chicago: Open Court, 1998.

Swami "M." *Gayatri Mantra*. Trans. A.K. Malhotra. Karnataka, India: Gale and Malhothra.

Takyi, H.K. and Kishin Khubchandani, eds. *Words of Jesus and Sathya Sai Baba*. Pune, India: Khubchandani.

Tuoti, Frank. *Why Not Be a Mystic?* New York, Crossroad, 1997.

Waxemberg, Jorge. *The Art of Living in Relationship*. New York: Cafh Foundation, 1994.

————. *Living Consciously*. New York: Cafh Foundation, 1996.

Whitmont, Edward Christopher and Sylvia Brinton Perera. *Dreams, a Portal to the Source*. New York: Routledge, 1989.

Ullman, Montague. "Access to Dreams" in B. Wolman and M. Ullman, eds. *Handbook of States of Consciousness*. New York: Van Nostrand Reinhold, 1986.

Note: Most of the books on Sai Baba are available from the Sathya Sai Book Center of America, Tustin, CA.

Of Related Interest...

Revised & Expanded
In the Presence of Mystery
An Introduction to the Story of Human Religiousness
Michael H. Barnes

This book goes to the very core of religious belief and practice, ranging from preliterate to modern culture. It helps readers understand that the call to be human includes the religious response.

376 pp, $24.95, 1-58595-259-1

Paradox
The Spiritual Path to Transformation
Bernard Tickerhoof

This book is meant for all those who struggle with belief at any time in their lives. Tickerhoof grounds the reader in the Christian experience by exploring both the life and death of Jesus, who embodies the challenge, the hope, and the fulfillment of paradox.

240 pp, $19.95, 1-58595-216-8

New Paths to God
Moving Forward on the Spiritual Journey
Catherine M. Harmer

The author suggests some paths to a closer relationship with God, a deeper sense of the sacred, and a fuller meaning to life—in other words, a spirituality for today.

128 pp, $10.95, 1-58595-154-4

Seven Days with the Gospel of John
A Personal Retreat
Joseph G. Donders

Donders offers meditations for both morning and evening, as well as points for prayer and application. The reader will follow Jesus as he is seen by so many others: in his moments of teaching, healing, suffering, and glory. In so doing readers will be drawn into their own faith story.

64pp, $6.95, 1-58595-254-0

TWENTY-THIRD PUBLICATIONS
185 WILLOW STREET • PO BOX 180 • MYSTIC, CT 06355
TEL: 1-800-321-0411 • FAX: 1-800-572-0788
E-MAIL: ttpubs@aol.com • www.twentythirdpublications.com